Country
Ground Beef

No question—ground beef is the No. 1 meat on country dinner tables. It's convenient, affordable and good-tasting! But most country cooks would agree that finding new and interesting ways to prepare it can be a challenge.

It won't be a challenge for *you* any longer, though!

Country Ground Beef offers hundreds of deliciously different recipes to "beef up" your family's menus. Choose from a variety of outstanding appetizers...mouth-watering meat loaves...old-fashioned oven meals... sure-to-please pizzas...filling soups and sandwiches...sizzling skillet suppers...and a hearty helping of Mexican meals!

From Phyllis Miller's "Meatball Vegetable Soup" (see page 10) to Marilyn Leum's "Golden Secret Meat Loaf" (see page 29 for "secret" ingredient), some 300 imaginative recipes will break menu monotony in your household— without doing the same to your budget!

That's because ground beef is an inexpensive mainstay of country appetites. But best of all, the family-proven favorites in *Country Ground Beef* come from the personal recipe files of great cooks all across the country.

So turn the page...and turn your next pound of ground beef into a savory, satisfying "seconds, please" dish today!

Editor: Linda Piepenbrink
Food Editor: Mary Beth Jung
Assistant Food Editor: Coleen Martin
Test Kitchen Assistant: Denise Simeth
Assistant Editors: Kristine Krueger, Patty Kishpaugh, Dawn Verkuilen
Art Directors: Ellen Lloyd, Stephanie Marchese
Cover Design: Stephanie Marchese
Food Photography: Mike Huibregtse, Judy Anderson

©1993, Reiman Publications, L.P.
5400 S. 60th St., Greendale WI 53129
International Standard Book Number: 0-89821-188-3
Library of Congress Catalog Card Number: 93-83939
All rights reserved.
Printed in U.S.A.

Country Ground Beef

CONTENTS

❖ ❖ ❖

Pictured on the cover. Clockwise from top: Minestrone (p. 11), French Meat Pie (p. 67), Italian Spaghetti and Meatballs (p. 70), Grilled Hamburgers (p. 9).

Appetizers

SNAPPY COCKTAIL MEATBALLS
Nancy Means, Moline, Illinois
(PICTURED AT LEFT)

This recipe was given to me over 20 years ago by a German lady. They're easy to prepare and can be made ahead of time.

    2 pounds lean ground beef
    2 eggs, beaten
1-1/4 cups fresh bread crumbs
    1 teaspoon salt
1/2 teaspoon garlic salt
1/2 teaspoon onion powder
1/2 teaspoon pepper
SAUCE:
    1 can (28 ounces) tomatoes with liquid, chopped
1/2 cup packed brown sugar
1/4 cup vinegar
1/2 teaspoon salt
    1 teaspoon grated onion
   10 gingersnaps, finely crushed

Place first seven ingredients in large mixing bowl; mix well. Shape into 1-1/4-in. balls. Place on ungreased baking sheets. Bake at 450° for 15 minutes. Drain on paper towels. Meanwhile, for sauce, combine tomatoes, brown sugar, vinegar, salt and onion in large saucepan or Dutch oven. Bring to a boil. Add gingersnaps; mix well, continuing to boil until sauce is thick and clear. Reduce heat to simmer; add meatballs. Heat through. **Yield:** about 5 dozen.

PIZZA FONDUE
Susan D. Carlson, Perry, New York
(PICTURED AT LEFT)

I heard about this recipe on a talk show, then "personalized" it by using my own home-canned spaghetti sauce.

    1 onion, chopped
1/2 pound ground beef
    3 cans (8 ounces *each*) pizza sauce
    1 tablespoon cornstarch
1-1/2 teaspoons dried oregano
1/4 teaspoon garlic powder
    1 cup (4 ounces) shredded cheddar cheese, *divided*
1-1/2 teaspoons fennel seed
    1 cup (4 ounces) shredded mozzarella cheese
    1 loaf French bread, cubed

In heavy saucepan, brown onion and beef; drain off fat. Stir in pizza sauce, cornstarch, oregano and garlic powder; mix well. Add 1/2 cup cheddar cheese; stir until the cheese melts. Gradually add remaining cheddar cheese; blend until smooth. Pour into fondue pot. Add fennel seed and mozzarella cheese, stirring until melted. Serve with cubed French bread. **Yield:** 10-12 servings.

ORIENTAL TRIANGLES
Violet Heaton, Portland, Oregon
(PICTURED AT LEFT)

Crunchy vegetables, savory meat and a flaky crust—there's a lot to like in these little pockets!

1/2 pound lean ground beef
    1 envelope (1 ounce) beef and mushroom dry soup mix
1/2 cup sliced water chestnuts, finely chopped
    1 cup canned bean sprouts, drained
    2 tablespoons chopped onion
    2 tubes (8 ounces *each*) refrigerated crescent rolls
Prepared sweet-and-sour sauce, optional
Prepared hot mustard sauce, optional

In a skillet, combine first five ingredients. Cook over medium heat, stirring often, until beef is browned and onion is tender. Separate crescent dough into triangles; cut each one in half diagonally. Place 1 rounded teaspoon of beef mixture in center of each triangle; fold dough over mixture and pinch corners together to seal edges. Place on ungreased baking sheet. Bake at 375° for 15 minutes or until golden. Serve with sweet-and-sour sauce and hot mustard sauce if desired. **Yield:** about 3 dozen.

CHEESEBURGER BITES
Holly Camozzi, Petaluma, California
(PICTURED AT LEFT)

This is a recipe from my mother. I like to make up a batch or two and store in the freezer till I'm ready to cook them.

    1 egg yolk, beaten
1/2 pound lean ground beef
    2 tablespoons grated onion
1/2 teaspoon salt
Dash pepper
    6 slices bread
   24 cubes cheddar cheese (1/2-inch cubes)

In a mixing bowl, combine egg yolk, ground beef, onion, salt and pepper. Shape mixture by teaspoonfuls into 24 balls. Remove crusts from bread; roll flat and cut into 1-1/2-in. rounds. Place meatballs on bread rounds; make a depression in each ball and fill with a small cube of cheese, making sure bread is covered with meat mixture. Place on baking sheet. Broil in preheated oven about 6 inches from heat for 3-5 minutes or until no pink remains. Garnish with ketchup, mustard, sliced green onions or sliced dill pickles if desired. **Yield:** 2 dozen.

BEEFY BITEFULS. Pictured at left from top to bottom: Snappy Cocktail Meatballs, Pizza Fondue, Oriental Triangles and Cheeseburger Bites (all recipes on this page).

Beef 'n' Cheddar Biscuits
Della Jackson, Loomis, California

This was a winning recipe at the county fair when I was a child. It's a family favorite—and great picnic fare.

    1 pound ground beef, browned and
        drained
    4 tablespoons bottled barbecue sauce
    2 tubes (4-1/2 ounces *each*) refrigerated
        biscuits
    1 cup (4 ounces) shredded cheddar cheese

Combine ground beef and barbecue sauce in a small bowl; set aside. Place one biscuit in each of 12 greased muffin cups; press firmly into the bottom and up the sides. Spoon 1-2 tablespoons of beef mixture into each cup; sprinkle with cheese. Bake at 350° for 15-18 minutes or until biscuits are golden and cheese is melted. Serve immediately. **Yield:** 1 dozen.

Chilaquilas
Joy Frost, Wood River, Illinois

I learned how to make this recipe when I was attending high school in California. It's been a family favorite for years.

    1 pound ground beef
Salt and pepper to taste
    1 to 2 tablespoons chili powder
    6 green onions with tops, sliced
    1 can (6 ounces) pitted ripe olives, sliced
    1 can (16 ounces) tomatoes with liquid,
        chopped
    1 can (16 ounces) chili beans, undrained
    1 package (20 ounces) tortilla *or* corn chips
    1 to 2 cups (4 to 8 ounces) shredded
        cheddar cheese

In a skillet, brown meat; drain. Add salt, pepper, chili powder, onions, olives, tomatoes and beans. Simmer until thickened, about 20 minutes. Arrange chips on a platter; top with meat mixture and sprinkle cheese on top. Serve immediately. **Yield:** 8-10 servings.

Spicy Party Meatballs
Sue Yaeger, Brookings, South Dakota

These spicy meatballs are great served with fresh veggies for a nice change of pace.

    1-1/2 pounds ground beef
    1-1/2 cups soft bread crumbs
    1/2 medium onion, chopped
    1/3 cup milk
    1/4 cup chopped fresh parsley
    1/2 teaspoon pepper
        1 egg, beaten
        1 pound Mexican *or* regular process
            cheese, cubed
        1 can (4 ounces) chopped green chilies
        1 package (1-1/4 ounces) taco seasoning

In a mixing bowl, combine first seven ingredients; mix well. Shape into 1/2-in. balls. Cook in a skillet over medium-high heat 2-3 minutes or until browned;

drain. In a saucepan, combine cheese, green chilies and taco seasoning; stir until well blended and the cheese melts. Add meatballs; cover and simmer until heated through. **Yield:** 8-10 servings.

Chili Con Queso Dip
Tammy Leiber, Navasota, Texas

I can count on a roomful of smiles whenever I make this—and it couldn't be easier!

    1 pound ground beef
    1 medium onion, chopped
    1 to 2 teaspoons chili powder, optional
    1/4 to 1/2 teaspoon garlic powder
    1 can (4 ounces) chopped green chilies
    1 tablespoon Worcestershire sauce
    2 cans (8 ounces *each*) tomato sauce
    1 pound process cheese, cubed
Tortilla *or* corn chips

In a large skillet, brown beef and onion; drain. Stir in remaining ingredients except chips. Cook over medium heat, stirring constantly until the cheese melts. Transfer to fondue pot or chafing dish. Serve warm with chips. **Yield:** 12 servings.

Hamburger-Broccoli Dip
Marvel Maki, Ponca City, Oklahoma

Here's an appetizer that's guaranteed to keep hunger pangs at bay until dinner's ready!

    1 package (10 ounces) frozen chopped
        broccoli
    1/2 pound ground beef
    1/2 teaspoon salt
    1 pound process cheese, cubed
    1 can (10 ounces) tomatoes with green
        chilies
Corn chips

Cook broccoli according to package directions; drain and set aside. In a skillet, brown ground beef and salt; drain off fat. Add cheese; cook and stir until cheese is melted. Add tomatoes and broccoli; mix well. Serve with chips. **Yield:** 8-10 servings.

Chili Cheese Dip
Nancy Brown, Janesville, Wisconsin

I love to keep these ingredients on hand for entertaining or quick-to-prepare hearty snacks.

    1/4 to 1/2 pound ground beef
    1 can (15 ounces) chili con carne without beans
    1 pound process cheese, cubed
    1 can (4 ounces) chopped green chilies
Tortilla chips

In a saucepan, brown ground beef; drain. Add chili, cheese and green chilies. Heat over medium-low, stirring frequently, until cheese melts. Serve warm with chips. **Yield:** 12 servings.

SOUTH OF THE BORDER DIP

Sandy Robideau, Eureka, Montana

Sometimes I double the recipe and serve it as a meal with chopped tomato, sliced avocados and sliced black olives.

    1/2 pound ground beef
      1 can (15-1/2 ounces) refried beans
      1 can (8 ounces) tomato sauce
      1 package (1-1/4 ounces) taco seasoning
      1 small onion, finely chopped
    1/2 green pepper, finely chopped
    1/2 teaspoon dry mustard
    1/2 teaspoon chili powder
SOUR CREAM TOPPING:
      1 cup (8 ounces) sour cream
      2 tablespoons shredded cheddar cheese
    1/4 teaspoon chili powder
GARNISH:
      2 cups shredded lettuce
      1 cup (4 ounces) shredded cheddar cheese
Tortilla chips

Brown beef; drain. Stir in beans, tomato sauce, taco seasoning, onion, green pepper, mustard and chili powder. Bring to a boil, stirring constantly. Spread mixture into an ungreased 9-in. pie plate. Combine topping ingredients; spread over beef mixture. Sprinkle with lettuce and cheese. Serve with chips. **Yield:** 3-1/2 cups.

FIESTA APPETIZERS

Sharon Skildum, Maple Grove, Minnesota

The fact that these go from freezer to oven means less last-minute kitchen fuss…and more time to spend with guests!

      1 pound ground beef
      1 pound bulk pork sausage
      1 medium onion, chopped
      1 pound Mexican-style process cheese, cubed
      1 tablespoon Worcestershire sauce
      1 teaspoon dried oregano
Salt and pepper to taste
      1 loaf (1 pound) sliced party rye bread

In a skillet, cook beef and sausage with onion until meat is browned and onion is tender; drain well. Stir in the cheese, Worcestershire sauce and seasonings. Spread rye bread slices with 1 heaping tablespoon of mixture; set aside. Just before serving, broil 3 minutes or until hot and bubbly. May be frozen and broiled without defrosting. **Yield:** about 4 dozen.

BARBECUED MEATBALLS

Mrs. Melvin Schnuelle, Manitowoc, Wisconsin

This is always a hit with guests—and with me, too, because it's simple and can be assembled ahead of time.

      1 pound lean ground beef
    1/2 cup dry bread crumbs
    1/3 cup minced onion
    1/4 cup milk
      1 egg, beaten

      1 tablespoon snipped fresh parsley
      1 teaspoon salt
    1/2 teaspoon pepper
      1 teaspoon Worcestershire sauce
    1/4 cup shortening
      1 bottle (12 ounces) chili sauce
      1 jar (10 ounces) grape jelly

In a mixing bowl, combine the first nine ingredients. Shape into 1-in. balls. Melt shortening in a large skillet; brown meatballs on all sides. Remove meatballs and drain fat. In same skillet, combine chili sauce and jelly. Heat over medium, stirring constantly, until jelly has melted. Return meatballs to skillet; heat through. Serve warm in a chafing dish. **Yield:** about 5 dozen.

TACO TARTLETS

Mary Little, Richardson, Texas

The bright colors in these zippy little tarts make any gathering a festive one. They freeze well, too.

FILLING:
      1 cup (8 ounces) sour cream
      2 tablespoons taco sauce
      3 tablespoons chopped ripe olives
      1 cup coarsely crushed tortilla chips
MEAT SHELLS:
      1 pound ground beef
      2 tablespoons taco seasoning
      2 tablespoons water
      1 cup (4 ounces) shredded cheddar cheese

In a mixing bowl, combine filling ingredients; set aside. In another bowl, combine beef, taco seasoning and water; mix well. Press into bottom and sides of mini-muffin cups. Place a teaspoonful of filling into each meat shell; sprinkle with cheese. Bake at 425° for 7-8 minutes or until beef is cooked and filling is bubbly. Remove immediately from pan. Serve warm. **Yield:** about 2 dozen.

SWEET-AND-SOUR MEATBALLS

Gigi Trapp, Mt. Carmel, Illinois

My sister served these meatballs as a holiday treat one year. Now, when I make them, someone always asks for the recipe.

      2 cups soft bread crumbs
    1/2 cup milk
    1/2 pound lean ground beef
    1/2 pound bulk pork sausage
      1 can (8 ounces) water chestnuts, finely chopped
      1 tablespoon soy sauce
    1/2 teaspoon garlic powder
    1/4 teaspoon onion salt
Prepared sweet-and-sour sauce, optional

Combine bread crumbs and milk in small bowl; set aside. Meanwhile, combine ground beef, sausage, water chestnuts, soy sauce, garlic powder and onion salt. Add to bread crumb mixture; mix well. Form into 1-1/2-in. meatballs. Place on baking sheet; bake at 350° for about 20 minutes. Serve with sweet-and-sour sauce if desired. **Yield:** 3-4 dozen.

Soups & Sandwiches

TACO SOUP

Debbie Moffitt, Albany, Oregon
(PICTURED AT LEFT)

My family—husband Dave and I and our three teenagers—enjoy this spicy, hearty soup. It's a nice change of pace from regular soups and it's also fast to make.

      1 pound ground beef
      1 envelope (1-1/4 ounces) taco seasoning
      1 can (14-1/2 ounces) stewed tomatoes
      1 can (15 ounces) kidney beans, undrained
      1 cup water
Shredded cheddar cheese (about 1/4 cup per serving)
Sliced green onions, sour cream and corn *or* tortilla chips for garnish, optional

Brown ground beef in a large Dutch oven. Drain fat. Add taco seasoning, tomatoes, beans and water; heat until soup comes to a boil and is heated through. Ladle into individual bowls; top with cheese. If desired, also top with onions, corn chips and sour cream. **Yield:** 5 cups.

JANE'S CHILI

Jane Seeling, Keene, New Hampshire

Served with hot homemade bread, this makes a delicious meal on a cold day. If you prefer dishes that are mild or if you don't have green chilies on hand, this soup is also good without them.

      1 pound dried kidney beans
      9 cups water
  1-1/2 pounds ground beef
      1 large onion, chopped
      3 cans (16 ounces *each*) stewed tomatoes
      1 can (29 ounces) tomato puree
      2 cans (4 ounces *each*) green chilies
      3 garlic cloves, minced
  1/8 cup dried parsley flakes
      1 tablespoon dried red pepper flakes
      1 tablespoon dried oregano
      2 teaspoons ground cumin
Salt and pepper to taste

Rinse beans. Place in a Dutch oven or soup kettle; cover with water and bring to a boil. Boil 2 minutes. Remove from the heat; let stand 1 hour. Drain beans and discard liquid. In the same kettle, bring beans and water to a boil. Reduce heat and simmer for 1-1/2 to 2 hours or until tender. Drain (beans should measure 6 cups) and set aside. In a large skillet, brown beef and onion. Drain fat. Combine beans, beef/onion and all re-

maining ingredients in a kettle or Dutch oven. Simmer for about 1 hour. **Yield:** 6-8 servings.

STUFFED ROAST PEPPER SOUP

Betty Vig, Viroqua, Wisconsin
(PICTURED AT LEFT)

After sampling a similar soup at a summer resort, my daughter and I invented this version. Using a colorful variety of peppers gives it plenty of eye appeal.

      2 pounds ground beef
  1/2 medium onion, chopped
      6 cups water
      8 beef bouillon cubes
      2 cans (28 ounces *each*) tomatoes with liquid, cut up
      2 cups cooked rice
      2 teaspoons salt
  1/2 teaspoon pepper
  1/2 teaspoon paprika
      3 green, yellow *or* sweet red peppers, seeded and chopped

In a large Dutch oven or soup kettle, cook ground beef with onion until the meat is brown and the onion is tender; drain. Add water, bouillon, tomatoes, rice and seasonings. Bring to a boil; reduce heat and simmer, covered, for 1 hour. Add chopped peppers; cook, uncovered, for 10-15 minutes or just until tender. **Yield:** 14-16 servings (4 quarts).

GRILLED HAMBURGERS

Marcille Meyer, Battle Creek, Nebraska
(PICTURED AT LEFT)

Even when I know we won't be eating all eight burgers, I make the whole recipe and freeze the leftovers already grilled. Warmed in the microwave, they make a quick meal and taste fresh off the grill!

      2 pounds lean ground beef
  1/2 cup quick-cooking *or* rolled oats
  1/4 cup milk
      1 egg, beaten
  1/4 cup ketchup
  1/2 cup chopped onion
      3 teaspoons finely diced green pepper
      1 teaspoon salt
Dash pepper
      8 hamburger buns
Lettuce leaves, optional
Sliced tomato, optional

Combine first nine ingredients in a large bowl and mix well. Shape into eight patties. Grill until burgers reach desired doneness. Serve on buns with lettuce and tomato if desired. **Yield:** 8 servings.

> **FRESH AND FILLING.** Pictured at left, clockwise from top: Taco Soup, Stuffed Roast Pepper Soup and Grilled Hamburgers (recipes on this page).

9

■ ■ ■

CHUCK WAGON CHOWDER

Regina Somerlot, Wabash, Indiana

Serve fresh fruit or a salad with this hearty chowder and you have a complete meal! My family really enjoys it.

  1-1/2 **pounds ground beef**
    1 **small onion, diced**
    1 **package (10 ounces) frozen peas, thawed**
    3 **cans (14-1/2 ounces *each*) tomatoes with liquid, cut up**
    1 **quart plus 1 cup tomato juice**
    1 **package (1 pound) noodles**
    1 **teaspoon salt**
  1/2 **teaspoon dried basil**
  1/4 **teaspoon pepper**
    1 **to 2 cups (4 to 8 ounces) shredded American cheese**

In a skillet, brown beef with onion. Drain fat. Stir in peas, tomatoes and tomato juice. Add noodles and seasonings. Cover and cook on medium heat for 15 minutes, stirring as needed. Reduce heat and simmer for another 10-15 minutes. Sprinkle cheese on top and let it melt before serving. **Yield:** 8-10 servings.

■ ■ ■

MEATBALL VEGETABLE SOUP

Phyllis Miller, Hunta, Ontario

My daughter shared this favorite recipe with me. The meatballs make it different from usual vegetable soup recipes.

    1 **pound ground beef**
    1 **egg, lightly beaten**
  1/2 **cup small bread cubes**
  3/4 **cup finely chopped onion, *divided***
  1/2 **teaspoon salt**
    2 **tablespoons cooking oil**
    1 **can (10-3/4 ounces) beef broth**
    1 **can (10-3/4 ounces) condensed tomato soup, undiluted**
    1 **cup cooked small shell macaroni**
    1 **cup frozen peas, thawed**
  1/4 **teaspoon dried thyme**

In a large bowl, mix beef, egg, bread cubes, 1/4 cup onion and salt. Shape into 36 meatballs. Heat oil in a kettle or Dutch oven; brown meatballs with remaining onion. Add broth, soup, macaroni, peas and thyme; heat through, stirring often. **Yield:** 6 servings (6 cups).

■ ■ ■

TRULY TEXAN CHILI

Betty Brown, San Antonio, Texas

I am a native Texan, and this is the best chili recipe I've ever tasted—it's meaty and spicy. I'd make this whenever I was "homesick" during the years we spent away from Texas due to my husband's military career.

    2 **tablespoons cooking oil**
    3 **pounds ground beef**
    2 **to 3 garlic cloves, minced**
    3 **tablespoons chili powder (or to taste)**
    1 **tablespoon ground cumin**

  1/4 **cup all-purpose flour**
    1 **tablespoon dried oregano**
    2 **cans (14-1/2 ounces *each*) beef broth**
    1 **teaspoon salt**
  1/4 **teaspoon pepper**
    1 **can (15 ounces) pinto beans, drained, optional**
Optional garnishes: shredded cheddar cheese, tortilla chips, sour cream *and/or* lime wedges

Heat oil in a large kettle or heavy saucepan. Brown beef, stirring frequently, until no longer pink. Drain fat. Reduce heat; stir in garlic. Combine chili powder, cumin, flour and oregano; sprinkle over meat, stirring until evenly coated. Add broth, salt and pepper; bring to a boil, stirring occasionally. Reduce heat; cover and simmer for 1-1/2 to 2 hours, stirring occasionally. (Chili can be transferred to a slow cooker for simmering if desired.) Cool. Cover and refrigerate overnight. Reheat in a heavy saucepan, double boiler or slow cooker over low heat. If desired, add beans and heat through. Garnish individual bowls, if desired, with cheese, tortilla chips, sour cream and/or lime wedges. **Yield:** 4-6 servings (5 cups).

■ ■ ■

GERMAN VEGETABLE SOUP

Gudrun Braker, Burnett, Wisconsin

My sister-in-law gave me this recipe—it's a nice thick soup. It does call for quite a few ingredients, but the taste is worth it!

  1-1/2 **pounds ground beef**
    2 **medium onions, diced**
    2 **tablespoons beef bouillon granules**
    1 **cup water**
Salt and pepper to taste
  1/2 **to 1 teaspoon garlic powder**
    1 **bay leaf**
    1 **can (46 ounces) tomato *or* vegetable juice**
    3 **celery stalks, diced**
    6 **carrots, sliced**
    3 **medium potatoes, peeled and diced**
    3 **cups shredded cabbage**
    1 **small green pepper, chopped**
    1 **can (8 ounces) cut green beans, drained**
    1 **can (8-1/2 ounces) sweet peas, drained**
    1 **can (15 to 16 ounces) whole kernel corn, drained**

In a large kettle or Dutch oven, brown beef and onions. Drain fat. Dissolve bouillon in water; add to kettle. Add salt, pepper, garlic powder, bay leaf, tomato juice, celery, carrots, potatoes, cabbage and green pepper; simmer until vegetables are tender, about 25 minutes. Stir in beans, peas and corn; heat through. Remove bay leaf before serving. **Yield:** 16 servings (4 quarts).

■ ■ ■

QUICK CHILI

Betty-Jean Molyneux, Geneva, Ohio

This recipe is handy when you want a fast, filling meal.

    1 **pound ground beef**
    1 **cup diced onion**
    2 **cans (15 ounces *each*) kidney beans, partially drained**

2 cans (16 ounces *each*) tomatoes with
   liquid, cut up
1 celery stalk, diced
1 teaspoon salt
1 teaspoon pepper
1/2 teaspoon chili powder (or to taste)
1/4 to 1/2 teaspoon crushed red pepper

In a large saucepan or skillet, brown beef with onion until meat is no longer pink. Drain fat. Add beans and tomatoes. Add remaining ingredients and bring to a boil. Reduce heat and simmer for at least 30 minutes. **Yield:** 6 servings (2 quarts).

SOUP IN A HURRY
Eleanor Holmes, Fairview, Oklahoma

Serve up this soup with corn bread and fruit and you have a delicious and simple supper.

2 pounds ground beef, browned and drained
2 cans (10-3/4 ounces *each*) condensed
   minestrone soup, undiluted
2 cans (15 ounces *each*) chili beans with gravy
1 can (16 ounces) Mexican-style *or* regular
   stewed tomatoes
1/2 to 1 cup mild, medium *or* hot picante sauce

In a large saucepan, combine all ingredients. Mix well and bring to a boil. Reduce heat and simmer for 20-30 minutes. **Yield:** 8-10 servings (10 cups).

MINESTRONE
Virginia Bauer, Botkins, Ohio
(PICTURED ON COVER)

Vegetables and herbs fresh from my garden make this one of our favorite soups. This recipe makes a lot, so it's perfect for large gatherings or to freeze in smaller containers for fast meals.

1-1/2 pounds ground beef
2 cups coarsely chopped onion
1 cup sliced celery
1/4 cup chopped fresh parsley
2 garlic cloves, minced
1/4 cup cooking oil
5 cups beef broth *or* bouillon
2 cups fresh chopped tomatoes *or* 1 can
   (16 ounces) tomatoes with liquid, cut up
1 can (15 ounces) tomato sauce
2 cups coarsely chopped cabbage
1 cup sliced carrots
2 teaspoons dried basil *or* Italian seasoning
1/2 teaspoon salt
1/4 teaspoon pepper
1-1/2 cups sliced zucchini
1 cup cut green beans
1 can (15-1/2 ounces) kidney beans, undrained
1 can (16 ounces) garbanzo beans, undrained
4 ounces uncooked spaghetti (2- to 3-inch
   pieces) *or* 1 cup uncooked elbow macaroni
1 cup grated Parmesan cheese

In a skillet, brown ground beef. Drain and set aside. In an 8-qt. kettle, saute onion, celery, parsley and garlic

in oil until tender. Stir in next eight ingredients and bring to a boil. Reduce heat; cover and simmer for 1 hour. Stir in cooked beef, zucchini, all three beans and spaghetti. Simmer, covered, for 15-20 minutes or until vegetables are tender and spaghetti is cooked. Spoon into individual bowls and top with Parmesan cheese. **Yield:** 20 servings (about 5 quarts).

THREE-BEAN SOUP
Marilyn Coy, St. Helena, California

This is a terrific recipe for cold days. Even my young son asks for it! I like it because it's so easy to fix.

1 pound ground beef
1 can (28 ounces) tomatoes with liquid, cut up
1 can (10-1/2 ounces) condensed beef
   consomme, undiluted
1 cup water
1/2 cup pearl barley
1/4 cup chopped onion
1 teaspoon salt
1/4 teaspoon dried marjoram
1/4 teaspoon dried thyme
1 can (16 ounces) cut green beans *or*
   Italian-style green beans, drained
1 can (16 ounces) dark red kidney beans,
   drained
1 can (16 ounces) lima *or* wax beans, rinsed
   and drained
Grated Parmesan *or* Romano cheese, optional

In a large kettle, brown beef. Drain fat. Add tomatoes, consomme, water, barley, onion, salt, marjoram and thyme; bring to a boil. Reduce heat; cover and simmer for 50 minutes. Stir in all beans and bring to a boil. Reduce heat and simmer for 10 minutes. If desired, sprinkle individual bowls with grated cheese. **Yield:** 8-10 servings (9 cups).

TACO JOES
Marjorie Nolan, Oakland, Illinois

Here's a quick way to spice up ordinary burgers—our family sure enjoys the change of pace.

1 pound ground beef
1 can (16 ounces) tomatoes with liquid,
   cut up
1 teaspoon Worcestershire sauce
1 to 2 teaspoons chili powder
1 teaspoon garlic salt
1/2 teaspoon dry mustard
1/2 teaspoon ground cumin
1/2 teaspoon sugar
8 hamburger buns, split and toasted
1 cup (4 ounces) shredded cheddar cheese
2 cups shredded lettuce

Brown beef in a skillet; drain fat. Add tomatoes, Worcestershire sauce and seasonings. Stir well and bring to a boil. Reduce heat; simmer, uncovered, for 15-20 minutes or until thickened. Spoon onto buns and top with cheese and lettuce. Serve immediately. **Yield:** 8 servings.

CHUCK WAGON CHOW. Clockwise from top: Calico Chili (p. 14), Sicilian Burgers (p.15), Cheeseburger Broccoli Chowder (p. 15), "Long Boy" Cheeseburgers (p. 14), Hamburger Vegetable Soup (p. 14) and Stromboli (p.14).

HAMBURGER VEGETABLE SOUP

Eleanor Bell, Utica, Pennsylvania
(PICTURED ON PAGE 12)

This filling soup is a favorite in our family and is fast to prepare. It is the one food I take most often to friends who are sick or have lost a loved one.

      1 pound ground beef
      1 cup chopped onion
      1 cup diced peeled potatoes
      1 cup sliced carrots
      1 cup shredded cabbage
      1 cup sliced celery
      2 cans (16 ounces *each*) tomatoes with
         liquid, cut up
  1/4 cup uncooked long grain rice
      3 cups water
      2 teaspoons salt
  1/4 teaspoon dried basil
  1/4 teaspoon dried thyme
      1 bay leaf

In a large soup kettle or Dutch oven, brown beef and onion until the meat is no longer pink. Drain excess fat. Add all remaining ingredients and bring to a boil. Reduce heat; cover and simmer for 1 hour, stirring occasionally. Remove bay leaf before serving. **Yield:** 8 servings (2 quarts).

CALICO CHILI

Camille Gouldsborough, Grosse Isle, Manitoba
(PICTURED ON PAGE 13)

I developed this recipe myself when I was 16. It freezes well and almost tastes better the day after you make it. The variety of vegetables make it colorful to serve and give it the calico name.

      1 pound ground beef
      1 medium onion, chopped
      2 garlic cloves, minced
      1 celery stalk, chopped
      1 green pepper, chopped
      1 cup diced zucchini, optional
      1 tablespoon chili powder (or to taste)
      1 tablespoon dried parsley flakes
  1/4 teaspoon *each* dried oregon, thyme and
         rosemary
Salt and pepper to taste
      1 can (30 ounces) kidney beans, drained
      1 can (15 to 16 ounces) whole kernel corn,
         drained
      1 can (28 ounces) tomatoes with liquid,
         cut up
      1 cup cooked rice
      1 cup water
      2 tablespoons vinegar
      1 tablespoon Worcestershire sauce

In a large kettle or Dutch oven, brown ground beef. Drain. Add onion, garlic, celery and green pepper. Also add zucchini if desired. Cook until onion is transparent. Add spices. Stir in remaining ingredients; sim-

mer, stirring occasionally, until thickened and vegetables are heated through, about 20 minutes. **Yield:** 8-10 servings (10 cups).

"LONG BOY" CHEESEBURGERS

Edna Carolyn Griffin, Macon, Georgia
(PICTURED ON PAGE 12)

This flavorful sandwich is fast to prepare and makes a complete meal with a salad.

      1 pound extra-lean ground beef
      1 teaspoon salt
      1 teaspoon pepper
      1 tablespoon Worcestershire sauce
  1/4 cup ketchup
  1/4 cup chopped onion
  1/2 cup crushed cornflakes
  1/2 cup whipping cream
      2 loaves brown 'n' serve French bread
      1 cup (4 ounces) shredded cheddar cheese

In a 2-qt. bowl, mix together first eight ingredients. Cut each loaf of bread in half lengthwise; spread one-fourth of meat mixture over each half, covering all the way to edges. Place on baking sheet. Bake at 350° for about 25 minutes, or until meat is cooked, sprinkling with cheese during the last 5 minutes of baking. Cut into slices to serve. **Yield:** 8 servings.

STROMBOLI

Erma Yoder, Millersburg, Indiana
(PICTURED ON PAGE 12)

Feeding teenagers is what this recipe is perfect for! It freezes well, so it's handy to quickly reheat in the microwave.

      1 package (1/4 ounce) active dry yeast
  1-1/3 cups warm water (110°-115°)
  1/4 cup vegetable oil
  1/2 teaspoon salt
      4 to 5 cups all-purpose flour
FILLING:
      3 tablespoons prepared mustard
      12 slices process American cheese
      12 slices hard salami
  1-1/2 pounds ground beef, browned and
         drained
  1/2 pound thinly sliced cooked ham
      4 cups (16 ounces) shredded mozzarella
         cheese
Vegetable oil
Oregano to taste

Dissolve yeast in water in a large bowl. Add oil, salt and flour. Turn out onto a lightly floured surface and knead until smooth and elastic, about 10 minutes. Place in a greased bowl, turning once to grease top. Cover and let rise in a warm place until doubled, about 45 minutes. Divide dough in half; roll one half into a 15-in. x 12-in. rectangle. Spread half of rectangle with half of mustard. Over mustard, layer six slices of cheese and salami, and half of the beef, ham and mozzarella. Fold plain half of dough over filling and seal ends well. Brush with oil and sprinkle with oregano. Repeat with other half of dough and remaining filling ingredients. Bake at 400° for 25-30 minutes or until lightly browned. Cool slightly before cutting into 1-in. slices. **Yield:** about 16 servings.

■ ■ ■

TERIYAKI BURGERS
Rose Thusfield, Holcombe, Wisconsin

The teriyaki sauce takes these cheeseburgers from "ordinary" to "oh, boy"! Look for this sauce in the Chinese food section of your grocery store.

2 medium onions, sliced
1/2 cup teriyaki sauce
1 pound lean ground beef
4 slices mozzarella *or* farmer cheese
Hamburger rolls

In a skillet, saute onions in teriyaki sauce until tender. Shape ground beef into four patties; place on top of onions and cook on both sides to desired doneness. Top each burger with cheese and onions. Serve on rolls. **Yield:** 4 servings.

■ ■ ■

SICILIAN BURGERS
Beverly Gordon, Rapid City, South Dakota
(PICTURED ON PAGE 13)

The unique flavor of these burgers make them a favorite of my family's. They're also good reheated as leftovers.

1-3/4 pounds ground beef
1 cup chopped onion
1-1/4 cups ketchup
1/4 cup dill relish
1/2 teaspoon salt
1/4 teaspoon dried basil
1/8 teaspoon pepper
1-1/2 cups (6 ounces) shredded process cheese
12 hamburger buns

Brown beef and onion in a skillet. Drain fat. Remove from the heat; stir in ketchup, relish, salt, basil and pepper and mix well. Stir in cheese. Spread meat mixture onto buns. Wrap sandwiches individually in foil and place in a baking pan. Heat at 325° for 15-20 minutes or until the cheese melts. **Yield:** 12 servings.

■ ■ ■

CHEESEBURGER BROCCOLI CHOWDER
Karen Davies, Wanipigow, Manitoba
(PICTURED ON PAGE 13)

I invented this recipe accidentally! Actually, it came about when I was new to cooking, and didn't know that "chowder" was a kind of soup—so I made mashed potatoes to go with the dish I was making. We ended up dunking our mashed potatoes into the soup as "gravy"—and it was delicious!

1/2 pound ground beef
1/2 cup chopped onion
1/4 cup chopped green pepper

1 can (11 ounces) condensed cheddar cheese soup, undiluted
1 soup can milk
1 teaspoon Worcestershire sauce
1 cup chopped broccoli
1 to 2 potatoes, peeled and diced

In a large saucepan, cook beef with onion and green pepper until the beef is browned and the vegetables are tender; drain. Stir in soup, milk and Worcestershire sauce. Add broccoli and potatoes. Bring to a boil, reduce heat and simmer, covered, about 30 minutes or until the potatoes are tender. **Yield:** 4 servings.

■ ■ ■

TACO BURGERS
Linda Logan, Warren, Ohio

My family loves the taste of tacos, but I dislike the mess! So I developed these burgers as a tasty but "neat" alternative.

1-1/2 pounds ground beef
1 tablespoon instant minced onion
1 envelope (1-1/4 ounces) taco seasoning mix
1 cup finely crushed corn chips
1 egg, beaten
6 slices cheddar cheese
Hamburger buns
Lettuce leaves
Tomato slices
Salsa, optional

In a mixing bowl, combine beef, onion, seasoning mix, corn chips and egg; mix well. Shape into 6 patties. Broil or grill to desired doneness. Top each burger with a slice of cheese; continue cooking until cheese just begins to melt. Serve on hamburger buns with lettuce, tomato and salsa, if desired. **Yield:** 6 servings

■ ■ ■

SWISSCAMOLE BURGERS
Dlores DeWitt, Colorado Springs, Colorado

This recipe won the Chef Award at a contest sponsored by a major food company more than 20 years ago. Since then, it's the burger recipe my husband and I like best.

1 pound lean ground beef
1-1/2 teaspoons salt, *divided*
1/4 teaspoon pepper
2 ripe avocados
1 tablespoon grated onion
1 tablespoon lemon juice
1/3 cup mayonnaise
4 bacon strips, cooked and crumbled
4 slices Swiss cheese
4 hamburger buns

In a mixing bowl, combine ground beef with 1/2 teaspoon salt and pepper. Shape into 8 small patties. Mash avocados and mix with remaining salt, onion, lemon juice, mayonnaise and bacon. Place a slice of cheese on 4 of the patties. Top with avocado mixture. Cover with another pattie; press edges to seal. Broil or grill to desired doneness. Serve on toasted buns. **Yield:** 4 servings.

■ ■ ■
SLOPPY JOES
Dorothy Wiedeman, Eaton, Colorado

This is a little spicier version of the traditional sloppy joes. They're easy to make and perfect for parties—the recipe could easily be increased.

- 1 pound ground beef
- 1 garlic clove, minced
- 1/2 medium onion, chopped
- 2 to 3 celery stalks, sliced
- 1/3 cup chopped green pepper
- 1/4 cup chili sauce
- 1/4 cup ketchup
- 1 cup water
- 3/4 teaspoon salt
- 1/8 teaspoon pepper
- 1 tablespoon Worcestershire sauce
- 2 tablespoons vinegar
- 2 teaspoons brown sugar
- 1 teaspoon dry mustard
- 1/2 teaspoon paprika
- 1/2 teaspoon chili powder
- 1 tablespoon dried parsley flakes
- 6 to 8 hamburger buns

In a large saucepan or Dutch oven, brown ground beef, garlic and onion. Drain fat. Add celery and green pepper. Add all remaining ingredients except buns; bring to a boil. Reduce heat and simmer for 1 hour. Spoon onto buns. **Yield:** 6-8 servings (3 cups).

■ ■ ■
BURGERS FOR A BUNCH
Nancy C. Latham, Moses Lake, Washington

I used to make this often when my children were small and I worked full-time. It's easy to prepare the night before, then pop into the oven shortly before suppertime. We still like it— even as a cold snack!

FILLING:
- 1 pound ground beef
- 1/2 cup chopped onion
- 1 teaspoon salt
- 1/4 teaspoon pepper
- 3/4 cup instant potato flakes
- 1 egg, beaten
- 1/4 cup ketchup
- 1/4 cup hamburger relish
- 1 tablespoon prepared mustard
- 1/2 cup shredded cheddar cheese

CRUST:
- 1/2 cup butter *or* margarine, *divided*
- 1/2 cup instant potato flakes, *divided*
- 2 cups all-purpose flour
- 1 tablespoon sugar
- 1 teaspoon cream of tartar
- 1 teaspoon baking soda
- 1/2 cup milk
- 1/4 cup mayonnaise

Additional milk

In a large skillet, brown ground beef with onion, salt and pepper until meat is browned and onion is tender. Drain. Stir in potato flakes, egg, ketchup, relish and

mustard; set aside. For crust, melt 2 tablespoons butter in a small saucepan. Stir in 1/4 cup potato flakes; set aside. In a mixing bowl, combine remaining potato flakes, flour, sugar, cream of tartar and baking soda. Cut in remaining butter; add milk and mayonnaise. Blend until a soft dough forms. Divide in half. On a floured surface, roll one portion of dough into a 10-in. circle. Place in a 9-in. pie pan. Spread with meat filling; sprinkle with cheese. Roll out remaining dough and place on top of filling. Seal and flute edges. Brush with milk; sprinkle with reserved buttered potato mixture. Bake at 375° for 20-25 minutes or until golden brown. Cut into wedges to serve. **Yield:** 6-8 servings.

■ ■ ■
CALICO MAIN DISH SOUP
Josie Pritchard, Atkinson, Illinois

Serve this hearty soup with a pan of corn bread on a cold winter's night…it'll warm you right down to your toes!

- 1-1/2 pounds ground beef
- 1/2 cup diced green pepper
- 1/3 cup chopped onion
- 2 tablespoons chili powder
- 1 teaspoon ground cumin
- 1 teaspoon salt
- 2 cans (10-3/4 ounces *each*) condensed golden mushroom soup, undiluted
- 1 soup can of water
- 1 can (16 ounces) tomatoes with liquid, cut up
- 1 can (15 to 16 ounces) whole kernel corn, drained
- 1 can (15-1/2 ounces) green beans, drained
- 1 cup uncooked instant rice
- 1 to 2 cups tomato juice, optional

In a 4-qt. saucepan, brown ground beef; drain. Add green pepper, onion, chili powder, cumin and salt. Cook and stir over medium heat 5 minutes. Add soup, water, tomatoes, corn, beans and rice. Bring to a boil; reduce heat and simmer 20 minutes, stirring occasionally. Thin with tomato juice if desired. **Yield:** 6-8 servings (2 quarts).

■ ■ ■
HAMBURGER CHOWDER
Stephanie Allread, Bradford, Ohio

To add extra variety to this easy soup, toss in whatever leftovers you have on hand. This recipe is quick to assemble, a definite plus here on our small but busy livestock farm.

- 1 pound ground beef
- 1 small onion, chopped
- 2 cups diced peeled potatoes
- 1 cup chopped carrots
- 1 cup chopped celery
- 1 can (28 ounces) tomatoes with liquid, cut up
- 2 cups water
- 2 cups tomato juice
- 1/2 cup pearl barley
- 1 tablespoon dried parsley flakes *or* 3 tablespoons chopped fresh parsley

1/2 teaspoon dried oregano
2 teaspoons salt
1/2 teaspoon pepper

In a large Dutch oven or soup kettle, cook ground beef with onion until meat is browned and onion is tender; drain. Add remaining ingredients. Bring to a boil; reduce heat and simmer, covered, for 1-1/2 hours, stirring occasionally. **Yield:** about 10 cups.

■ ■ ■

PRAIRIE BEAN SOUP

Katherine VanDeraa, South Bend, Indiana

This soup started out as an "end-of-the-month" meal, a creative way to use up items that were on hand. We liked it so well that I now prepare it even when the pantry is full. My twin daughters and I all enjoy cooking...and my husband reaps the benefits!

1 pound ground beef
1 pound bulk pork sausage
2 large onions, chopped
1/2 cup packed brown sugar
1 tablespoon ground cumin
1/2 teaspoon garlic powder
1 tablespoon prepared mustard
1 cup ketchup
1/2 cup water
1/3 cup vinegar
4 cups cooked and drained pinto beans
2 cans (15 ounces *each*) chili beans
2 cans (16 ounces *each*) pork and beans
1 tablespoon salt
1-1/2 teaspoons pepper

In a large Dutch oven or soup kettle, cook ground beef with pork sausage and onions until the meat is browned and the onions are tender; drain well. Stir in the next seven ingredients; mix well. Stir in beans, salt and pepper. Bring to a boil; reduce heat and simmer for about 2 hours. **Yield:** 12-16 servings (4 quarts).

■ ■ ■

CABBAGE SOUP

Nancy Stevens, Morrison, Illinois

My husband was never too fond of cabbage...until the first time he tried this recipe from my aunt. Now he even asks me to make this soup!

1 cup chopped celery
1 cup chopped onion
1 medium head cabbage, chopped
8 cups water
1 beef bouillon cube
1 tablespoon salt
2 teaspoons pepper
1-1/2 pounds ground beef, browned and drained
2 cans (15 ounces *each*) tomato sauce
1 tablespoon brown sugar
1/4 cup ketchup

In a large Dutch oven or soup kettle, cook the celery, onion and cabbage in water until tender. Add bouillon, salt, pepper, beef and tomato sauce. Bring to a boil; reduce heat and simmer 10 minutes. Stir in brown sugar

and ketchup; simmer another 10 minutes or until heated through. **Yield:** 16-20 servings (5 quarts).

■ ■ ■

BEEF AND BACON CHOWDER

Marilyn Yost, Livingston, California

My mother discovered this recipe while I was still a child, and we loved it! To save time, I sometimes cook the carrots and potatoes in the microwave. Either way, this chowder is perfect for a family supper and special enough for company.

12 bacon strips, cut into 1-inch pieces
1 pound ground beef
2 to 3 cups diced celery
1/2 cup diced onion
2 cans (10-3/4 ounces *each*) condensed cream of mushroom soup, undiluted
4 cups milk
3 to 4 cups diced peeled potatoes, cooked and drained
2 cups carrots, cooked and drained
2 teaspoons salt
1 teaspoon pepper
Fresh chopped parsley

In a large skillet, cook bacon until crisp; pour off drippings and remove bacon to paper towel to drain. In the same skillet, cook ground beef with celery and onion until the beef is browned and the vegetables are tender; drain. Add soup, milk, potatoes, carrots, bacon, salt and pepper. Bring to a boil; reduce heat and simmer until heated through. Garnish with parsley. **Yield:** 10-12 servings.

■ ■ ■

HEARTY STEAK SOUP

Waldeane Logan, Butler, Missouri

My husband and I live in a small farming community and we've been married for more than 40 years, so I've been cooking for a long time. Our granddaughters love to come and help me cook—especially when the result is this soup. We like it with toasted French bread and a crisp salad for a complete meal.

1/2 cup butter *or* margarine
1 cup all-purpose flour
6 cups water
2 pounds ground round steak *or* ground beef, browned and drained
1 cup chopped onion
1 cup chopped celery
1 package (20 ounces) frozen mixed vegetables, thawed
1 can (28 ounces) tomatoes with liquid, cut up
1 tablespoon seasoned salt
1 teaspoon salt
1 teaspoon pepper
2 tablespoons bottled browning sauce

In a large saucepan, melt butter. Stir in flour to make a smooth paste. Add water; cook and stir over medium heat until thickened. Add beef, onion, celery, mixed vegetables, tomatoes, seasonings and browning sauce. Bring to a boil; reduce heat and simmer 20-30 minutes or until the vegetables are tender. **Yield:** 8-10 servings (4 quarts).

■ ■ ■
BEEF STROGANOFF SANDWICH
Julie Terstriep, Industry, Illinois
(PICTURED AT LEFT)

This filling sandwich was a winner in our local beef cook-off several years ago. It's always been one of my favorites.

        2 pounds ground beef
    1/2 cup chopped onion
        1 teaspoon salt
    1/2 teaspoon garlic powder
    1/2 teaspoon pepper
        1 loaf French bread
Butter *or* margarine, softened
        2 cups (16 ounces) sour cream
        2 tomatoes, seeded and diced
        1 large green pepper, diced
        3 cups (12 ounces) shredded cheddar cheese

In a skillet, brown ground beef and onion. Drain. Stir in salt, garlic powder and pepper. Cut bread lengthwise in half; butter both halves and place on cookie sheets. Add sour cream to meat mixture; spoon onto bread halves. Sprinkle with tomatoes and green pepper and top with cheese. Bake at 350° for 20 minutes or until cheese is melted (bake longer for crispier bread). **Yield:** 8-10 servings.

■ ■ ■
MINESTRONE MIX-UP
Katherine Lewis, Carlsbad, New Mexico

On a cold day, there's nothing better than this soup with crusty homemade bread. I am a seamstress with three children. My husband and I enjoy fishing, camping, hunting...and eating!

        1 pound fresh spinach, washed, trimmed and finely chopped
    1/2 cup seasoned dry bread crumbs
        1 egg
    1/2 teaspoon salt
    1/4 teaspoon pepper
  1-1/2 pounds ground beef
        1 to 2 tablespoons cooking oil
        1 large onion, chopped
        1 can (16 ounces) tomatoes with liquid, cut up
  1-1/2 cups chopped celery
        1 cup sliced carrots
        1 can (16 ounces) kidney beans, rinsed and drained
    1/2 teaspoon dried oregano
    1/2 teaspoon dried basil
        8 cups water
        1 cup uncooked elbow macaroni
Tomato juice, optional

In a bowl, combine spinach, bread crumbs, egg, salt and pepper; add beef and mix well. Shape into 1-in. balls. Heat oil in a Dutch oven or large soup kettle; brown meatballs on all sides. Remove and keep warm.

HOT AND HEARTY. Pictured at left, clockwise from the bottom: Spicy Potato Soup, Beef Stroganoff Sandwich and Beef Barley Soup (all recipes on this page).

Add onion; cook and stir until tender. Add tomatoes, celery, carrots, beans, spices and water. Bring to a boil; reduce heat and simmer 20 minutes. Stir in macaroni and meatballs; cook 15 minutes longer or until the meatballs are cooked and the macaroni is tender. If soup is too thick, thin with tomato juice if desired. **Yield:** 8-10 servings (2-1/2 quarts).

■ ■ ■
SPICY POTATO SOUP
Audrey Wall, Industry, Pennsylvania
(PICTURED AT LEFT)

This recipe originally came courtesy of my sister-in-law, who is from Mexico. But since she prefers her foods much spicier than we do, I've cut back on the "heat" by reducing the amount of hot pepper sauce.

        1 pound ground beef
        4 cups cubed peeled potatoes (1/2-inch cubes)
        1 small onion, chopped
        3 cans (8 ounces *each*) tomato sauce
        4 cups water
        2 teaspoons salt
  1-1/2 teaspoons pepper
    1/2 to 1 teaspoon hot pepper sauce

In a large Dutch oven or soup kettle, brown ground beef; drain. Add potatoes, onion and tomato sauce. Stir in water, salt, pepper and hot pepper sauce. Bring to a boil; reduce heat and simmer 1 hour or until the potatoes are tender and the soup has thickened. **Yield:** 6-8 servings (2 quarts).

■ ■ ■
BEEF BARLEY SOUP
Maggie Norman, Stevensville, Montana
(PICTURED AT LEFT)

I first tasted this soup when a friend served it to our family one day after church. It's now a favorite with our family, especially our three children.

        2 quarts water
        2 meaty beef soup bones
        2 beef bouillon cubes *or* 2 teaspoons beef bouillon granules
        1 pound ground beef
    1/4 to 1/2 cup medium pearl barley
        1 large carrot, diced
        1 small onion, chopped
        3 to 4 medium potatoes, peeled and diced
        2 teaspoons garlic salt
        1 teaspoon onion powder
        2 teaspoons dried parsley
        1 teaspoon salt
        1 teaspoon pepper

In a large Dutch oven or soup kettle, bring water and soup bones to a rapid boil; add bouillon. Stir in ground beef in small amounts. Reduce heat; cover and simmer 1-1/2 hours or until the meat comes easily off the bones. Remove bones. Strain broth; cool and chill. Skim off fat. Remove meat from bones; dice and return to broth along with remaining ingredients. Bring to a boil. Reduce heat; cover and simmer about 1 hour or until vegetables are tender. **Yield:** 10-12 servings (about 2 quarts).

CARROT CHOWDER

Wendy Wilkins, Prattville, Alabama
(PICTURED AT RIGHT)

My husband's grandmother passed this recipe on to us, and it's just wonderful—especially with a basket of warm, fresh bread on the side. This soup freezes well.

    1 pound ground beef, browned and
      drained
  1/2 cup chopped celery
  1/2 cup chopped onion
    1 cup chopped green pepper
2-1/2 cups grated carrot
    1 can (32 ounces) tomato juice
    2 cans (10-3/4 ounces *each*) condensed
      cream of celery soup, undiluted
1-1/2 cups water
  1/2 teaspoon garlic salt
  1/2 teaspoon dried marjoram
    1 teaspoon sugar
  1/2 teaspoon salt
Shredded Monterey Jack cheese

Combine all ingredients except the cheese in a large Dutch oven or soup kettle. Bring to a boil; reduce heat and simmer, uncovered, about 1 hour or until the vegetables are tender. Sprinkle each serving with cheese. **Yield:** 8-10 servings (10 cups).

PIZZA SOUP

Janet Beldman, London, Ontario
(PICTURED AT RIGHT)

This family favorite is done in no time at all. I like to serve it with a crusty bread or garlic bread, and I'll sometimes use bacon or salami instead of pepperoni (just like a pizza!).

    1 pound ground beef, browned and drained
    1 small onion, chopped
    1 cup sliced mushrooms
    1 green pepper, cut into strips
    1 can (28 ounces) tomatoes with liquid,
      cut up
    1 cup beef broth
    1 cup sliced pepperoni
    1 teaspoon dried basil
Shredded mozzarella cheese

In a large saucepan, cook beef, onion, mushrooms and green pepper until meat is browned and vegetables are almost tender. Stir in tomatoes, broth, pepperoni and basil. Cook until heated through. Ladle into ovenproof bowls; top with cheese. Broil or microwave until cheese melts and is bubbly. **Yield:** 4-6 servings (6 cups).

PUMPKIN SLOPPY JOES

Eleanor McReynolds, Scott City, Kansas
(PICTURED AT RIGHT)

When my oldest granddaughter gave me eight of the 50 pumpkins she grew in her backyard, I didn't know how I'd use them all up! Then I remembered this recipe from a dear friend...I'm glad I tried it. I froze some of the pumpkin to use in this and other recipes, and also froze some of the sloppy joe mixture to enjoy later.

    1 pound ground beef
  1/2 cup chopped onion
    1 garlic clove, minced
    1 cup canned pumpkin
    1 can (8 ounces) tomato sauce
    2 tablespoons brown sugar
    2 tablespoons prepared mustard
    2 teaspoons chili powder
  1/2 teaspoon salt
    8 hamburger buns, split
American cheese slices

In a large skillet or saucepan, brown ground beef. Drain fat. Add onion and garlic; cook until tender. Stir in the pumpkin, tomato sauce, brown sugar, mustard, chili powder and salt. Bring to a boil. Reduce heat and simmer for 10 minutes. Meanwhile, if desired, cut cheese slices into shapes (triangles, half-circles, etc.) to make pumpkin faces. Spoon meat mixture onto buns; top with cheese shapes. Broil just until cheese melts. Serve immediately with bun top off to side. **Yield:** 8 servings.

HAMBURGER FLORENTINE SOUP

Mary Gillespie, Hollister, Missouri

I devised this recipe by adding herbs and spices to a dish in a recipe book that I received as a wedding present. It's a delicious way to serve spinach.

    1 pound ground beef
    5 cups water
    2 cups cubed peeled potatoes
    1 cup shredded cabbage
    1 cup chopped onion
    2 beef bouillon cubes
    1 cup sliced celery
    1 cup sliced carrot
  1/3 cup pearl barley
1-1/2 teaspoons salt
  1/2 teaspoon dried basil
  1/2 teaspoon dried thyme
  1/4 teaspoon pepper
    1 bay leaf
    1 can (28 ounces) tomatoes with liquid, cut up
    1 can (16 ounces) cut green beans,
      undrained
    1 package (10 ounces) frozen spinach,
      chopped

In a Dutch oven or soup kettle, brown ground beef; drain. Stir in remaining ingredients except spinach; bring to a boil. Reduce heat; cover and simmer 40 minutes. Add spinach; cover and simmer an additional 15 minutes. Stir to blend spinach into soup. Remove bay leaf before serving. **Yield:** 10-12 servings (14 cups).

AUTUMN ATTRACTIONS. Pictured at right, clockwise from the bottom: Carrot Chowder, Pizza Soup and Pumpkin Sloppy Joes (all recipes on this page).

CLASSIC GERMAN HAMBURGERS
Virginia Biehler, Fremont, Ohio

The bit of nutmeg in the meat mixture adds a subtle Old World flavor to these patties. Serve them with your favorite potato recipe.

>   2 pounds lean ground beef
>   1 medium onion, minced
>   3 tablespoons minced fresh parsley
>   2 eggs, beaten
>   1/2 to 1 teaspoon salt
>   1/8 teaspoon pepper
>   1/8 teaspoon ground nutmeg
>   2 tablespoons all-purpose flour
>   2 tablespoons butter *or* margarine
>   2 large onions, thinly sliced, separated
>   into rings

In a large mixing bowl, combine ground beef, onion, parsley, eggs, seasonings and flour; mix well. Shape into six patties. Melt butter in a skillet; cook patties to desired doneness. Remove hamburgers to a serving platter and keep warm. Cook onion rings in pan juices until soft and golden. Spoon onions and remaining cooking juices over hamburgers. Serve immediately. **Yield:** 6 servings.

GREEN CHILI
Gloria Rhinehart, Albuquerque, New Mexico

This is the best chili I've ever had. It was handed down to me by mother, who learned it from her mother. We enjoy it with crackers or a pan of corn bread.

>   1 pound ground beef
>   1/2 cup chopped onion
>   1 can (14-1/2 ounces) stewed tomatoes
>   2 cans (4 ounces *each*) chopped green
>   chilies
>   2 cups diced peeled potatoes
>   2 cups water
>   1/2 teaspoon salt

In a Dutch oven or soup kettle, cook ground beef with onion until the beef is browned and the onion is tender; drain. Stir in tomatoes, green chilies, potatoes, water and salt. Simmer, uncovered, 45 minutes or until the potatoes are tender. **Yield:** 4-6 servings (5 cups).

FRONTIER CHOWDER
Maggie Rogers, Elizabethtown, Kentucky

The smoky hint of bacon in this chowder makes me think of cooking over a campfire; that's why I named it as I did. While it's simmering, I toss a salad and bake some biscuits for a meal that's ready in next to no time.

>   1 pound ground beef
>   1 medium green pepper, chopped
>   1 medium onion, chopped
>   1 can (10-3/4 ounces) condensed tomato
>   soup, undiluted

>   1 can (11-1/4 ounces) condensed bean with
>   bacon soup, undiluted
>   1 can (17 ounces) whole kernel corn,
>   drained
>   1 cup water

In a large saucepan, cook ground beef with green pepper and onion until the beef is browned and the vegetables are tender; drain. Stir in soups, corn and water. Cover and simmer 30 minutes to blend flavors. **Yield:** 6 servings (2 quarts).

THREE-STEP CHILI
Christine Perry, Denver, Colorado

This recipe comes from my grandmother, who—although of Irish descent—was considered one of the best Mexican-food cooks in western Oklahoma when I was growing up. Want to know her serving secret? Before you fill a serving bowl with the chili, rub the inside with a cut clove of garlic.

>   2 pounds ground beef
>   1 pound ground pork
>   4 cups water
>   1 can (8 ounces) tomato sauce
> Salt and pepper to taste
>   1 tablespoon instant dried onion
>   4 tablespoons chili powder
>   2 teaspoons ground cumin
>   1/4 to 1/2 teaspoon cayenne pepper
>   1 teaspoon dried minced garlic
>   1 teaspoon paprika
>   1 teaspoon dried oregano
>   1/4 cup white cornmeal
>   2 tablespoons all-purpose flour
> Water

In a large Dutch oven or soup kettle, brown ground beef and pork; drain well. Add water, tomato sauce, salt and pepper. Cover and simmer for 1-1/2 to 2 hours, adding more water if necessary. Stir in dried onion, chili powder, cumin, cayenne pepper, garlic, paprika and oregano. Simmer another 30 minutes. Combine cornmeal, flour and enough water to make a thin paste. Stir into chili. Simmer 10-15 minutes longer until slightly thickened. Thin with additional water if desired. **Yield:** 10-12 servings.

HEARTY HAMBURGER SOUP
Mrs. Ivan Hochstetter, Shipshewana, Indiana

Two generations of my family—so far!—have made this soup a cold-weather specialty.

>   1 pound ground beef
>   1 medium onion, chopped
>   2 cups tomato juice
>   1 cup diced carrot
>   1 cup diced peeled potato
>   1-1/2 teaspoons salt
>   1/4 teaspoon pepper
>   1 teaspoon seasoned salt
> WHITE SAUCE:
>   1/4 cup butter *or* margarine

1/3 cup all-purpose flour
4 cups milk

In a skillet, brown ground beef with onion until the beef is brown and the onion is tender; drain. Add tomato juice, carrot and potato. Stir in seasonings. Cover and simmer 10-15 minutes or until the vegetables are tender. Meanwhile, melt butter in a saucepan. Stir in the flour; cook and stir until smooth. Remove from heat; gradually stir in milk. Return to heat; cook and stir until thickened. Stir in vegetable mixture and cook until heated through. **Yield:** 4-6 servings (2 quarts).

PUMPKIN CHILI

Betty Butler, Greencastle, Indiana

This unique chili freezes well...but it still doesn't last around our farmhouse very long, especially when my five children and 13 grandchildren are around! They often are—we are a very close-knit family.

3 pounds ground beef
1 medium onion, chopped
1 cup canned pumpkin
1 teaspoon salt
1 teaspoon pepper
2 teaspoons pumpkin pie spice
2 cans (10-3/4 ounces *each*) condensed tomato soup, undiluted
2 cans (16 ounces *each*) hot chili beans
2 bottles (12 ounces *each*) chili sauce
1 teaspoon sugar
1 teaspoon chili powder

In a large Dutch oven or soup kettle, brown ground beef with onion; drain. Add remaining ingredients; stir to mix well. Add water if desired to reduce thickness. Bring to a boil; reduce heat and simmer 1 hour. **Yield:** 10-12 servings (11 cups).

HAM, BEEF AND BACON SOUP

Mrs. J.C. Mantel, Orange City, Iowa

I invented this recipe one evening when I wanted to serve soup, but had no time to shop—so I used whatever I had on hand. When my husband said, "Please make it again!", I hurriedly wrote down the ingredient list!

1/2 pound ground beef, browned and drained
1/2 pound bacon, diced, cooked and drained
1/2 pound fully cooked ham, cubed
2 cans (15 ounces *each*) butter beans, drained
1 medium onion, chopped
1 package (20 ounces) frozen mixed vegetables, thawed
1 can (10-1/2 ounces) condensed beef broth, undiluted
1 can (10-3/4 ounces) condensed tomato soup, undiluted
1 teaspoon sugar
3/4 teaspoon salt
1/4 teaspoon pepper
1 to 2 cups tomato juice, optional

In a Dutch oven or soup kettle, combine beef, bacon, ham, beans, onion, mixed vegetables, broth, soup, sugar, salt and pepper. Bring to a boil; reduce heat and simmer 30 minutes or until vegetables are tender. Season with additional salt and pepper if desired. If a thinner soup is preferred, stir in tomato juice. **Yield:** 10-12 servings (3 quarts).

BEST HOMEMADE CHILI

Ruby Callander, Elk Grove, California

I won a prize at the county fair with this recipe! We like our chili hot, so I add lots of red pepper...you can add as much or as little as you like.

4 pounds ground beef
2 large onions, diced
4 teaspoons chili powder
Crushed dried red pepper flakes to taste
2 teaspoons dried oregano
2 teaspoons ground cumin
2 teaspoons paprika
3 teaspoons garlic powder
2 large onions, diced
2 cans (one 15 ounces, one 29 ounces) tomato sauce
3 tablespoons all-purpose flour
2 tablespoons vinegar

In a large Dutch oven or soup kettle, brown beef with onions until the beef is brown and the onions are tender; drain. Stir in spices and tomato sauce. Simmer, uncovered, for 1 hour, stirring occasionally. Combine flour and vinegar; stir into chili. Simmer another 15 minutes or until thickened. **Yield:** 16-20 servings.

BROCCOLI, HAMBURGER AND CHEEESE SOUP

Gloria Cudmore, Castlewood, South Dakota

This is a meal in itself—it's both hearty and nutritious—and I usually serve it with just a simple salad and hard rolls.

1-1/2 cups water
2 chicken bouillon cubes
1 package (10 ounces) frozen broccoli
1/4 cup finely chopped onion
2 tablespoons butter *or* margarine
3 tablespoons all-purpose flour
1/4 teaspoon salt
1/8 teaspoon pepper
2 cups milk
1 cup cubed process cheese
1 pound ground beef, browned and drained

In a saucepan, bring water to a boil; add bouillon and stir until dissolved. Add broccoli; cook according to package directions. Do not drain. Remove from the heat; set aside. In a large saucepan, cook onion in butter until tender. Add flour, salt and pepper; stir until well blended. Remove from heat and stir in enough milk to make a smooth paste; stir in remaining milk. Return to heat; bring to a boil and boil 1 minute, stirring constantly. Add cheese, ground beef, broccoli and cooking liquid. Cook until heated through and the cheese is melted, stirring occasionally. Serve hot. **Yield:** 6 servings (6-1/2 cups).

■ ■ ■

POTATO BURGERS
Mary Arnold, Long Prairie, Minnesota

Some folks might call this recipe a form of Swedish potato sausage. I call it getting my meat and potatoes in one dish—deliciously!

   1 pound ground beef
   2 cups grated peeled potatoes
 1/2 cup chopped onion
 1/2 teaspoon salt
 1/4 teaspoon pepper
 1/4 cup water
Hamburger buns, optional

In a mixing bowl, combine beef, potatoes, onion, salt and pepper; mix well. Shape into six to eight patties. In a skillet, brown patties. Add water; simmer for 15 minutes or until patties are cooked through. Serve on hamburger buns, if desired, or as a breakfast sausage. **Yield:** 6-8 servings.

■ ■ ■

BEEF AND CHEESE LOAF
Diane Martin, Brown Deer, Wisconsin

Here's a really different way to enjoy the taste of a cheeseburger…only better!

   1 loaf (1 pound) unsliced white bread
1-1/2 pounds ground beef
   1 green pepper, chopped
   1 medium onion, chopped
   1 teaspoon salt
 1/2 teaspoon pepper
   1 tablespoon Worcestershire sauce
   1 can (11 ounces) condensed cheddar cheese soup, undiluted
   3 slices cheddar cheese

Cut off top of bread; hollow out remainder to form a shell and set shell aside. Cut the top and the bread removed from inside into cubes; set aside 2 cups. In a large skillet, brown beef; drain. Stir in green pepper, onion, seasonings and soup. Simmer 10 minutes. Stir in reserved bread cubes. Spoon into bread shell; top with cheese slices. Bake at 350° for 10 minutes. Cut into slices; serve immediately. **Yield:** 6 servings.

■ ■ ■

CHURCH SUPPER CHILI
Dorothy Smith, Napoleon, Ohio

We grow a lot of tomatoes and vegetables for canneries in our area—and for use in this original recipe of mine, which won first place in a "Best Chili" contest at work!

2-1/2 pounds ground beef
 1/2 cup chopped green pepper
   1 cup chopped celery
   2 cups chopped onion
   1 garlic clove, minced
   3 tablespoons chili powder
   2 teaspoons salt
 1/2 teaspoon pepper
   1 can (16 ounces) tomatoes with liquid, cut up
   1 can (46 ounces) tomato juice

   1 can (30 ounces) vegetable juice
   1 can (30 ounces) kidney beans, rinsed and drained
   1 can (30 ounces) hot chili beans

In a large Dutch oven or soup kettle, brown ground beef; drain. Add green pepper, celery, onion and garlic; cook until tender. Add spices, tomatoes and juices. Bring to a boil; reduce heat and simmer for 20 minutes. Add beans and simmer 20 minutes longer. **Yield:** 20-24 servings.

■ ■ ■

EASY CALZONE
Cindy Covey, Heuvelton, New York

During haying season, I bake this in my convection oven, which turns itself automatically. That way, dinner is ready and waiting when we walk in the door!

 3/4 pound ground beef
 1/2 cup chopped onion
   1 can (8 ounces) pizza sauce
 1/2 teaspoon dried basil
 1/2 teaspoon dried oregano
   4 hoagie rolls (about 6 inches long)
1-1/2 cups (6 ounces) shredded mozzarella cheese

In a skillet, brown beef with onion; drain. Stir in pizza sauce, basil and oregano; simmer for 5 minutes. Meanwhile, slice each roll lengthwise 1/2 in. from the top; set tops aside. Hollow out rolls to 1/2 in. of bottom and sides; discard. Sprinkle 3 tablespoons of cheese into each roll; spoon the meat sauce evenly into rolls. Sprinkle with remaining cheese. Replace tops of rolls. Wrap each roll individually in foil. Bake at 375° for 30 minutes or until heated through. **Yield:** 4 servings.

■ ■ ■

CHICKEN ESCAROLE SOUP WITH MEATBALLS
Norma Manna, Hobe Sound, Florida

This is an old recipe from southern Italy. My mother gave it to me when I was first married. It started out as a holidays-only dish…but my children and granchildren love it so much that we have it every chance we get!

 15 chicken wings
  4 medium carrots, cut into 1/2-inch pieces
  1 large potato, cut into 1/2-inch cubes
  4 celery stalks, sliced
  1 large tomato, seeded and diced
  1 large onion, diced
  1 tablespoon salt (or to taste)
  1 teaspoon pepper
  4 quarts water
  1 small head (about 5 to 6 ounces) escarole
MEATBALLS:
  1 egg, beaten
1/2 pound ground beef
1/2 cup dry bread crumbs
  1 tablespoon chopped fresh parsley
1/2 teaspoon salt
  1 garlic clove, minced

1 teaspoon grated Parmesan cheese

Combine first nine ingredients in a large Dutch oven or soup kettle. Bring to a boil; reduce heat and simmer, covered, 1 hour, or until the chicken and vegetables are tender. Remove chicken wings; discard bones and return meat to kettle. Add escarole; cook 15 minutes longer. For meatballs, combine all ingredients in a bowl; mix well. Shape into marble-sized balls; add to simmering soup. Cook for 10 minutes or until the meatballs are done. **Yield:** 22-24 servings (6 quarts).

— ⠿ ⠿ ⠿ —

AUTUMN SOUP
Irene Dee, Ogilvie, Minnesota

I received this recipe from my daughter Janet. It's a wonderful way to enjoy fall's bounty…and it freezes well, too.

    1 can (28 ounces) stewed tomatoes
    1 pound ground beef
    1 cup chopped onion
    1 cup diced carrot
    1 cup diced celery
    1 cup diced peeled potato
    1 cup diced peeled rutabaga
    1 bay leaf
  1/8 teaspoon dried basil
    4 cups water

Puree tomatoes in a blender or food processor; set aside. In a skillet, brown ground beef; drain. Stir in tomatoes and remaining ingredients. Bring to a boil; reduce heat and simmer 25-30 minutes or until the vegetables are tender. Discard bay leaf before serving. **Yield:** 8-10 servings (10 cups).

— ⠿ ⠿ ⠿ —

QUICK VEGETABLE BEEF SOUP
June Formanek, Belle Plaine, Iowa

I send my husband off to the farm every day with lunch in a cooler. It's hard to have a variety of meals, especially hot ones. But a thermos full of this speedy soup keeps him smiling till he returns home!

  1-1/2 pounds ground beef
    1/3 cup instant minced onion
      1 can (46 ounces) tomato juice
      2 beef bouillon cubes
      1 package (20 ounces) frozen mixed
        vegetables, thawed
      1 teaspoon sugar
    1/2 teaspoon pepper

In a Dutch oven or soup kettle, brown ground beef with onion; drain. Add remaining ingredients. Bring to a boil; reduce heat and simmer 20-30 minutes or until the vegetables are tender. **Yield:** 10-12 servings (10 cups).

— ⠿ ⠿ ⠿ —

PIZZA BUNS
Eleanor Martens, Rosenort, Manitoba

These taste especially good as a snack after an afternoon of cross-country skiing or snowmobiling. I prepare them before we go and pop them in the fridge, then just heat them when we get home!

    2 pounds ground beef
    1 cup chopped onion
    1 garlic clove, minced
    1 cup ketchup
  1/4 teaspoon dry mustard
  1/2 teaspoon dried oregano
    1 tablespoon Worcestershire sauce
    2 cans (4 ounces *each*) mushrooms, drained
Shredded mozzarella cheese
Buttered hamburger buns

In a skillet, brown ground beef with onion and garlic; drain. Combine the ketchup, mustard, oregano and Worcestershire sauce; stir into beef mixture. Add mushrooms and mix well. Simmer 15 minutes or until heated through. Spoon onto buttered hamburger buns; sprinkle with mozzarella cheese. Place on baking sheets; heat under broiler until cheese melts. **Yield:** 10-12 servings.

— ⠿ ⠿ ⠿ —

TASTY BEEF SANDWICHES
Laurie Roberts, Carroll, Nebraska

My mother passed this recipe to me. When it's time for silage chopping and I've got a crowd of men to feed for dinner, it's perfectly tasty—and perfectly quick.

  2-1/2 pounds ground beef
    1/2 cup chopped onion
    1/2 cup water
    3/4 cup ketchup
      4 teaspoons prepared mustard
      4 teaspoons horseradish
      4 teaspoons Worcestershire sauce
      2 teaspoons salt
Hamburger buns

In a large skillet, brown ground beef; drain. Add onion and water; simmer until onion is tender. Stir in remaining ingredients; simmer for 10 minutes. Serve on hamburger buns. **Yield:** 12-16 servings.

— ⠿ ⠿ ⠿ —

CURRIED BEEF PITA POCKETS
Mary Ann Kosmas, Minneapolis, Minnesota

If there's anyone in your family who thinks they won't like the taste of curry, serve this…they'll be a "curry lover" forever!

    1 pound ground beef
    1 medium onion, chopped
    1 garlic clove, halved
    1 tablespoon curry powder
  1/2 cup water
  1-1/2 teaspoons salt
    1/2 teaspoon sugar
    1/4 teaspoon pepper
      1 medium tomato, seeded and diced
      1 medium zucchini, diced
      4 pita pocket breads

In a skillet, brown ground beef with onion, garlic and curry; drain and discard garlic. Stir in water, salt, sugar and pepper. Cover and simmer 15 minutes. Add tomato and zucchini; cook just until heated through. Spoon meat mixture into pita breads. **Yield:** 4 servings.

Meat Loaves

COMPANY MEAT LOAF

Alice Hoffman, Perry, Iowa
(PICTURED AT LEFT)

I received this recipe years ago from my sister who lives in Idaho. It's a hit every time I serve it!

FILLING:
- 1/2 cup butter *or* margarine
- 1/2 cup minced onion
- 1/2 cup diced celery
- 6 slices toasted bread, cubed
- 1 egg, beaten
- 1/2 cup water
- 1/2 teaspoon poultry seasoning
- 1/2 teaspoon salt
- 1/4 teaspoon pepper

MEAT LOAF:
- 1-1/2 pounds lean ground beef
- 1 egg, beaten
- 2/3 cup evaporated milk
- 1/4 cup dry bread crumbs
- 1 teaspoon salt

In a skillet, melt butter over medium heat. Saute onion and celery until tender. In a large bowl, combine bread cubes with egg and water. Add cooked vegetables, poultry seasoning, salt and pepper. Mix lightly and set aside. In another large bowl, combine ground beef, egg, milk, bread crumbs and salt. Pat two-thirds of the meat mixture on bottom and up the sides to within 3/4 in. of the top of a 9-in. x 5-in. x 3-in. loaf pan. Spoon filling into meat shell; cover top with the remaining meat mixture and seal edges. Bake at 350° for 1 hour or until no pink remains. Drain. Let loaf stand for 10 minutes before serving. **Yield:** 6-8 servings.

DELUXE MEAT LOAF

Ruth Fisher, Kingston, Ontario
(PICTURED AT LEFT)

This is not only my family's favorite meat loaf recipe when I serve it hot for supper...it's also the highlight of our mid-day lunch when I slice cold leftovers for sandwiches.

- 2 pounds lean ground beef
- 2 eggs, beaten
- 1 cup dry bread crumbs
- 2/3 cup milk
- 1/2 cup chopped onion
- 3 tablespoons horseradish
- 1 teaspoon prepared mustard
- 1 teaspoon salt

MARVELOUS MAINSTAYS. Pictured at left, clockwise from bottom: Meat Loaf Cordon Bleu, Company Meat Loaf, Deluxe Meat Loaf (recipes on this page).

- 1/8 teaspoon pepper
- 1/2 cup chili sauce

In a large bowl, combine first nine ingredients and mix well. Press into a 9-in. x 5-in. x 3-in. loaf pan. Bake at 350° for 1 hour. Remove from oven; drain. Spoon chili sauce over loaf. Return to oven and bake 20 minutes longer or until no pink remains. **Yield:** 8-10 servings.

MEAT LOAF CORDON BLEU

Barb Jacobsen, Campbell, Nebraska
(PICTURED AT LEFT)

I'm a school counselor and mother of one young child. Even with my busy schedule, I can make this in the morning and pop it into the oven when I get home.

- 1 egg, beaten
- 1 envelope (1-1/2 ounces) meat loaf seasoning
- 1/2 cup tomato sauce
- 2 cups soft bread crumbs
- 2 pounds lean ground beef
- 8 thin slices fully cooked ham
- 8 thin slices Swiss cheese
- 1 can (4 ounces) sliced mushrooms, drained

In a large bowl, mix together egg, meat loaf seasoning, tomato sauce and bread crumbs. Add ground beef; mix well. On a piece of waxed paper, pat meat mixture into an 18-in. x 9-in. rectangle. Top with layers of ham, cheese and mushrooms. Roll rectangle, jelly-roll style, starting from narrow end. Pinch edges to seal. Place seam side down in a shallow baking pan. Bake at 350° for 1-1/4 hours or until no pink remains. Let stand several minutes before slicing. **Yield:** 8-10 servings.

POTATO MEAT LOAF

Sandra Fenn, Quincy, Illinois

We're a family of meat-and-potato lovers—and the spuds in this loaf add extra goodness and a more pleasing texture than plain meat. Try it yourself and see if you don't agree!

- 1 pound potatoes
- 1 egg, beaten
- 1 tablespoon Worcestershire sauce
- 2 teaspoons soy sauce
- 1 teaspoon salt
- 1/2 teaspoon pepper
- 1/2 teaspoon garlic powder
- 1 pound lean ground beef

Peel and grate potatoes; rinse and drain. In a large mixing bowl, combine potatoes, egg, Worcestershire sauce, soy sauce, salt, pepper and garlic powder. Add ground beef and mix well. Pat meat mixture into an 8-1/2-in. x 4-1/2-in. x 2-1/2-in. loaf pan. Bake at 350° for 1 hour or until no pink remains. Drain. **Yield:** 4-6 servings.

GRANDMA'S MEAT LOAF
Joan Frey, Spencer, Ohio

We love Grandma's version of meat loaf so much that we have it at Thanksgiving, Christmas and Easter—the holidays wouldn't be the same without it! It's just as good the next day, as a cold sandwich.

    1 egg, beaten
1/4 cup dry bread crumbs
    3 bacon strips, cut into 1/4-inch pieces
    1 small onion, chopped
    2 ounces cubed cheddar cheese
1/2 teaspoon seasoned salt
1/2 teaspoon pepper
1-1/2 pounds lean ground beef
1/2 pound bulk pork sausage

In a large bowl, combine egg, bread crumbs, bacon, onion, cheese, seasoned salt and pepper. Add beef and sausage; mix well. In a shallow baking pan, shape mixture into an 8-1/2-in. x 4-1/2-in. x 2-1/2-in. loaf. Bake at 350° for 1-1/4 hours or until no pink remains. Drain. Let stand a few minutes before serving. **Yield:** 8-10 servings.

FAVORITE MEAT LOAF
Etta Winter, Pavilion, New York

My grandmother gave me this recipe many years ago. The buttery flavor of the crushed crackers is what gives this meat loaf the special taste that our family says is best!

    2 eggs, beaten
    1 cup milk
2/3 cup finely crushed butter-flavored crackers
1/2 cup chopped onion
    1 teaspoon salt
1/2 to 3/4 teaspoon ground sage *or* poultry seasoning
1/8 teaspoon pepper
1-1/2 pounds lean ground beef
Green pepper rings, optional
Onion rings, optional

In a large bowl, combine eggs, milk, crushed crackers, onion, salt, sage or poultry seasoning and pepper. Add ground beef; mix well. Press mixture into an 8-1/2-in. x 4-1/2-in. x 2-1/2-in. loaf pan. Bake at 350° for 1-1/4 hours or until no pink remains. Garnish with green pepper and onion rings if desired. **Yield:** 6-8 servings.

FROSTED MEAT LOAF
Doris Ratcliff, Souffville, Ontario

Our children have all "flown the nest", but my husband and I still enjoy this easy-to-make meat loaf. It has a taste like shepherd's pie (only better!).

    1 egg, beaten
1/4 cup milk
1/2 cup soft bread crumbs
    1 small onion, chopped
1/4 teaspoon salt
1/4 teaspoon pepper
1/4 teaspoon paprika
    1 pound lean ground beef
1/4 pound lean ground pork
1/4 pound fully cooked ground ham
FROSTING:
    2 cups hot mashed potatoes
1/2 cup shredded cheddar cheese
1/2 teaspoon salt
1/4 teaspoon dry mustard
1/8 teaspoon pepper

In a large mixing bowl, combine the egg, milk, bread crumbs, onion, salt, pepper and paprika. Add ground beef, pork and ham; mix well. Pat meat mixture into a 7-1/2-in. x 3-3/4-in. x 2-1/4-in. loaf pan. Bake at 350° for 1 hour or until no pink remains. Drain. Invert meat loaf onto a heat-proof platter. In a bowl, combine frosting ingredients. Cover top and sides of meat loaf with frosting mixture. Place under a preheated broiler; broil until lightly browned. **Yield:** 6-8 servings.

MEAT MUFFINS
Judy Nelson, Padroni, Colorado

Since we're ranchers, we always have a supply of beef on hand. This dish makes up individual servings that are easy to reheat when chores take one or more of us past our usual suppertime.

    1 egg, beaten
    1 cup milk
    2 cups soft bread crumbs
    2 teaspoons salt
    1 teaspoon Worcestershire sauce
1/2 teaspoon dried thyme
1/4 teaspoon pepper
    2 pounds lean ground beef
    1 pound lean ground pork
TOPPING:
1/2 cup packed brown sugar
1/3 cup ketchup

In a large bowl, combine egg, milk, bread crumbs, salt, Worcestershire sauce, thyme and pepper. Add beef and pork; mix well. Divide mixture into 16 equal portions. Pat meat portions lightly into 2-1/2-in. muffin cups. Bake at 350° for 25 minutes. Carefully drain. In a small bowl, combine topping ingredients. Spoon topping over each meat muffin. Bake about 10 minutes more or until no pink remains. Let muffins stand a few minutes before serving. **Yield:** 16 servings.

SAUCY MEAT LOAVES
Agatha Vander Kooi, Portage, Michigan

I have served this many times to dinner guests, along with mashed potatoes, broccoli in cheese sauce, salad and homemade rolls. It can easily be doubled for a large group.

    2 eggs, beaten
1/2 cup milk
1/2 cup bread crumbs

1/2 cup chopped onion
1/2 cup chopped celery
1/2 cup chopped green pepper
1 teaspoon salt
1/8 teaspoon pepper
2 pounds lean ground beef
SAUCE:
1 can (15 ounces) tomato sauce
1 can (4 ounces) chopped mushrooms, drained
2 tablespoons brown sugar

In a large mixing bowl, combine eggs, milk, bread crumbs, onion, celery, green pepper, salt and pepper. Add ground beef; mix well. Shape into 10 individual loaves, using about 1/2 cup mixture for each. Place in a 13-in. x 9-in. x 2-in. baking dish. In a small bowl, combine the sauce ingredients. Pour over the loaves. Bake, uncovered, at 350° for about 40 minutes or until no pink remains. **Yield:** 10 servings.

■ ■ ■

JUICY ITALIAN MEAT LOAF

Aleta Balmes, Waukegan, Illinois

When it's barbecue season, I make this meat loaf right on the grill! Just cook it covered, for the amount of time indicated. It's mmm-good!

1 egg, beaten
1/2 cup rolled oats
1 cup vegetable juice
1 teaspoon dried oregano, *divided*
1 teaspoon salt
1/8 teaspoon pepper
1/2 cup chopped onion
1-1/2 pounds lean ground beef
1-1/2 cups (6 ounces) shredded mozzarella cheese
2 tablespoons grated Parmesan cheese

In a large bowl, combine egg, oats, vegetable juice, 1/2 teaspoon oregano, salt, pepper and onion. Add beef; mix well. Place mixture on a piece of waxed paper and shape into an 18-in. x 7-in. rectangle. Sprinkle mozzarella cheese over rectangle. Starting at narrow end, roll up meat, jelly-roll style. Seal edges. Place seam side down in an 8-1/2-in. x 4-1/2-in. x 2-1/2-in. loaf pan. Bake at 350° for 1 hour. Remove loaf from oven and sprinkle with Parmesan cheese and remaining oregano. Return to oven and bake 15 minutes longer or until no pink remains. **Yield:** 6-8 servings.

■ ■ ■

McINTOSH MEAT LOAF

Lynnette Nicholl, Gouverneur, New York

I grew up in the heart of McIntosh country, where apples were always finding their way into everything! They give ordinary meat loaf a refreshing new taste.

1 cup chopped onion
1 tablespoon butter *or* margarine
2-1/2 pounds lean ground beef
3 eggs, beaten
2 cups chopped peeled McIntosh apples

1-1/2 cups dry bread crumbs
1/4 cup ketchup
1 tablespoon prepared mustard
1 tablespoon dried parsley flakes
1-1/2 teaspoons salt
1/2 teaspoon pepper
1/4 teaspoon ground allspice

In a small skillet, saute onion in butter. In a large bowl, combine onion with remaining ingredients. Pat mixture into a 9-in. x 5-in. x 2-in. loaf pan. Bake at 350° for 1 hour. Remove from the oven; drain. Bake 30 minutes longer. Remove from oven; drain again if necessary. Let stand 15 minutes before serving. **Yield:** 8-10 servings.

■ ■ ■

CURRIED MEAT LOAF

Denise Kilbock, Balgonie, Saskatchewan

This savory loaf has three things going for it: Extra color, out-of-the-ordinary taste and a wonderful aroma when it's baking. Plus, it's so easy!

1 egg, beaten
1/3 cup milk
1/2 cup dry bread crumbs *or* rolled oats
1 garlic clove, minced
1 to 2 teaspoons curry powder
1 teaspoon ground cumin
1/2 teaspoon salt
1/2 teaspoon pepper
1 cup shredded carrots
1 medium onion, chopped
1-1/2 pounds lean ground beef

In a large bowl, combine egg, milk, bread crumbs or oats, garlic, curry powder, cumin, salt, pepper, carrots and onion. Add ground beef; mix well. Pat meat mixture into an 8-1/2-in. x 4-1/2-in. x 2-1/2-in. loaf pan. Bake at 350° for 1-1/4 hours or until no pink remains. **Yield:** 6-8 servings.

■ ■ ■

GOLDEN SECRET MEAT LOAF

Marilyn Leum, Westby, Wisconsin

The "secret" in this meat loaf is cheese—one of our state's claims to fame! This recipe was given to me by a very good college friend.

1 egg, beaten
1 cup applesauce
1-1/2 cups soft bread crumbs
1 medium onion, chopped
1/2 teaspoon ground nutmeg
1/2 teaspoon salt
1/4 teaspoon pepper
2 pounds lean ground beef
4 ounces cheddar cheese, cut into 1/2-inch cubes

In a large bowl, combine the egg, applesauce, bread crumbs, onion, nutmeg, salt and pepper. Add ground beef; mix well. Fold in cheese. Pat into a 9-in. x 5-in. x 3-in. loaf pan. Bake at 350° for 1-1/2 hours or until no pink remains. Drain. Let stand a few minutes before slicing. **Yield:** 8-10 servings.

MARILYN'S MEAT LOAF

Marilyn Gould, Belmont, Nova Scotia

Our family of five loves baked ham...so every time I make it, I set aside some thin slices to add delicious flavor to my special meat loaf.

    1 egg, beaten
  1/3 cup tomato juice
    1 cup soft bread crumbs
    1 tablespoon chopped fresh parsley
  3/4 teaspoon Italian seasoning
  1/2 teaspoon dried oregano
  1/2 teaspoon salt
  1/4 teaspoon pepper
  1/4 teaspoon garlic salt
1-1/2 pounds lean ground beef
    4 to 6 slices thinly sliced fully cooked ham
    1 cup (4 ounces) shredded mozzarella cheese
Mozzarella cheese slices

In a large bowl, combine egg, tomato juice, bread crumbs, parsley, Italian seasoning, oregano, salt, pepper and garlic salt. Add ground beef; mix well. On a piece of waxed paper, pat meat mixture into a 14-in. x 10-in. rectangle. Place ham slices on meat; sprinkle with shredded mozzarella cheese. Starting from narrow end, roll meat mixture jelly-roll style. Seal seam and end of the roll. Place seam side down in a shallow baking dish. Bake at 350° for 1-1/4 hours or until no pink remains. Drain. Cut mozzarella slices into triangles; place on top of loaf. Return to oven just until cheese begins to melt. **Yield:** 6-8 servings.

COUNTRY MEAT LOAF

Marcia Baures, Waukesha, Wisconsin

The tangy glaze bakes to a rich, dark brown that makes this meat loaf look every bit as good as it tastes!

  1/2 cup chopped onion
    1 tablespoon butter *or* margarine
    2 eggs, beaten
    1 cup milk
  3/4 cup quick-cooking *or* rolled oats
    1 tablespoon chopped fresh parsley
    2 teaspoons salt
  1/2 teaspoon dried savory
  1/4 teaspoon pepper
2-1/2 pounds lean ground beef
GLAZE:
  1/2 cup ketchup
    2 tablespoons brown sugar
  1/2 teaspoon bottled browning sauce
  1/4 teaspoon dry mustard

In a small skillet, saute onion in butter until transparent. In a large bowl, combine onion with eggs, milk, oats, parsley and seasonings. Add beef and mix well. Press into an 8-1/2-in. x 4-1/2-in. x 2-1/2-in. loaf pan lined with waxed paper. Refrigerate for 2 hours. Unmold loaf into a shallow baking pan. Bake at 350° for 30 minutes. Meanwhile, combine glaze ingredients. Remove loaf from oven; drain. Brush with some of the glaze. Return

to oven; bake 1 hour longer or until no pink remains, occasionally brushing with glaze. **Yield:** 10-12 servings.

BARBECUE MEAT LOAF

Kerry Bouchard, Shawmut, Montana

My husband and I first tasted this recipe when we were dinner guests at the home of some friends. We liked it so much that I took the recipe home—and it's been one of our favorite main dishes ever since!

SAUCE:
    1 can (8 ounces) tomato sauce
  1/2 cup packed brown sugar
  1/4 cup vinegar
    1 teaspoon dry mustard
MEAT LOAF:
    2 pounds lean ground beef
    2 eggs, beaten
    1 cup quick-cooking *or* rolled oats
    1 medium onion, chopped
    1 medium green pepper, chopped
1-1/2 teaspoons salt
    1 teaspoon pepper
    1 teaspoon poultry seasoning
    1 teaspoon dried parsley flakes

In a small bowl, combine sauce ingredients; set aside. In a large bowl, mix together meat loaf ingredients. Add half of the sauce to the meat loaf mixture; mix well. Press into a 9-in. x 5-in. x 3-in. loaf pan. Bake at 350° for 1 hour. Remove from oven; drain. Pour remaining sauce over loaf. Return to oven and bake 20 minutes longer or until no pink remains. **Yield:** 8-10 servings.

CREOLE MEAT LOAF

Linda Kornelson, Empress, Alberta

We may live in Canada, but the taste of this meat loaf says "New Orleans"! When bell peppers are in season, this is one of the best ways I know to enjoy their flavor.

    1 egg, beaten
  1/2 cup coarsely crushed saltine crackers
    1 can (5 ounces) evaporated milk
  1/2 cup chopped green pepper
  1/4 cup chopped onion
    1 teaspoon dry mustard
    1 teaspoon salt
  1/4 teaspoon pepper
1-1/2 pounds lean ground beef

SAUCE:
     1 can (10-3/4 ounces) condensed tomato
        soup, undiluted
     2 tablespoons ketchup
   1/2 teaspoon horseradish

Combine egg, crackers, milk, green pepper, onion, mustard, salt and pepper. Add ground beef; mix well. Press into an 8-1/2-in. x 4-1/2-in. x 2-1/2-in. loaf pan. Bake at 350° for 1-1/4 hours or until no pink remains. Drain. Let loaf stand in pan for 10 minutes. Meanwhile, in a small saucepan, combine sauce ingredients. Cook until heated through. Turn loaf out onto a serving platter. Spoon 1/2 cup hot sauce over loaf; serve remaining sauce with meat loaf. **Yield:** 6 servings.

------- ▪ ▪ ▪ -------

MATCHLESS MEAT LOAF
Lila Bane, Vandalia, Illinois

This is the only meat loaf recipe I make! Our whole family loves its sweet tangy hint of molasses and mustard.

     2 eggs, beaten
     3 tablespoons light molasses
     3 tablespoons vinegar
     3 tablespoons prepared mustard
   1/4 cup ketchup
     2 to 4 drops hot pepper sauce
     1 cup milk
   1/2 teaspoon dried oregano
     1 envelope (1 ounce) dry onion soup mix
     3 cups soft bread crumbs
   1/4 cup chopped fresh parsley
     3 pounds lean ground beef

In a large mixing bowl, combine eggs, molasses, vinegar, mustard, ketchup, hot pepper sauce, milk, oregano, onion soup mix, bread crumbs and parsley. Add ground beef; mix well. In a shallow baking pan, shape meat mixture into a 9-in. x 5-in. x 3-in. loaf. Bake at 350° for 1 hour and 40 minutes or until no pink remains. Drain. Let loaf stand 10 minutes before slicing. **Yield:** 12-15 servings.

------- ▪ ▪ ▪ -------

APPLE-RAISIN MEAT LOAF
Linda Miller, Lodi, California

You won't believe just how good this recipe is until you try it. We grow our own grapes and process them into raisins.

     2 eggs, beaten
   1/2 cup applesauce
     1 cup soft bread crumbs
     1 cup coarsely crushed saltine crackers
   1/2 cup chopped onion
   1/2 cup chopped peeled apple
   1/2 cup raisins
 1-1/2 teaspoons salt
   1/4 teaspoon pepper
   1/4 teaspoon garlic powder
     2 pounds lean ground beef

In a large bowl, combine first 10 ingredients. Add ground beef; mix well. Pat mixture into a 9-in. x 5-in. x 3-in. loaf pan. Bake at 350° for 1-1/4 hours or until no pink remains.

Drain. Let stand at room temperature for 5 minutes before serving. **Yield:** 8-10 servings.

------- ▪ ▪ ▪ -------

VEGETABLE MEAT LOAF
Audrey Armour, Thamesford, Ontario

The colorful vegetables give this loaf a festive look—and they add so much goodness! Baking it in a casserole gives my meat loaf a unique shape, too, just for something a little different. Our family likes mashed potatoes, soup or salad and biscuits with it.

 1-1/2 pounds lean ground beef
     1 egg, beaten
     1 cup bread crumbs
     2 cups shredded carrots
     1 medium onion, chopped
   1/2 cup chopped celery
   1/2 cup chopped green pepper
     1 can (10-3/4 ounces) condensed tomato
        soup, undiluted
     1 teaspoon salt
   1/2 teaspoon Worcestershire sauce
   1/4 teaspoon pepper
   1/4 teaspoon dry mustard
   1/8 teaspoon cayenne pepper

In a large bowl, combine ground beef, egg and bread crumbs. Add remaining ingredients and mix well. Pat mixture into a 1-1/2-qt. casserole. Bake at 350° for 1-1/4 hours or until no pink remains. Drain. Unmold loaf to serve. **Yield:** 6-8 servings.

------- ▪ ▪ ▪ -------

PIZZA LOAF
Ruth Tacoma, Falmouth, Michigan

I'll always be thankful for the help my mother-in-law gave me when I first moved out to the farm. The "sure-to-please" recipes made a big adjustment easier. After all, dinnertime is often the only time a farm family can spend together…the meals had better turn out! Thanks to recipes like this one, my meals have been a "hit" much more often than a "miss".

     1 egg, beaten
     1 can (8 ounces) pizza sauce
     3 cups cornflakes
     1 can (4 ounces) chopped mushrooms, drained
   1/4 cup chopped onion
 1-1/2 teaspoons salt
   1/4 teaspoon pepper
     2 pounds lean ground beef
     1 cup (4 ounces) shredded mozzarella
        cheese, *divided*

In a large bowl, mix egg, pizza sauce, cornflakes, mushrooms, onion, salt and pepper. Add ground beef; mix well. Pat half of the meat mixture into a 9-in. square pan. Sprinkle half of the mozzarella cheese over top. Cover with the remaining meat. Bake at 350° for 50 to 60 minutes or until no pink remains. Drain. Sprinkle with remaining cheese. Let stand a few minutes until cheese melts. Cut into squares to serve. **Yield:** 9 servings.

   CHEDDAR LOAF: Substitute a can of tomato sauce for pizza sauce and shredded cheddar cheese for mozzarella.

CARROT MEAT LOAF

Irene Knodel, Golden Prairie, Saskatchewan
(PICTURED AT RIGHT)

We love to take slices of this tasty loaf to the field during harvest season—I either bake it or cook it up quickly in the microwave—it's a real blessing during our busiest time of year.

        3 eggs, beaten
    1/2 cup milk
        1 envelope (1 ounce) dry onion soup mix
        1 cup dry bread crumbs
        2 cups shredded carrots
        2 pounds lean ground beef
    1/2 pound ground pork
GLAZE:
    1/2 cup ketchup
    1/4 cup packed brown sugar
        2 teaspoons prepared mustard

Combine eggs, milk, soup mix, bread crumbs and carrots. Add beef and pork; mix well. Shape mixture into a circle with a 9-in. diameter; form a 3-in. hole in the center of the circle. Place in a shallow baking pan. Bake at 350° for 1 hour. Drain. Combine glaze ingredients; spread over meat. Bake 10 minutes longer or until no pink remains. **Yield:** 10 servings. **Microwave Method:** Prepare and shape loaf as above. Place on a microwave-proof platter. Cover with waxed paper. Microwave on high for 16-18 minutes or until no pink remains, giving the dish a quarter turn every 3 minutes. Drain. Let stand 5 minutes. Meanwhile, in a custard cup, combine glaze ingredients. Spread half the glaze over meat loaf. Return to microwave on medium for 1 minute; remove. Cover remaining glaze with waxed paper and heat in microwave on medium for 1 minute. Serve glaze in center of meat loaf.

POT ROAST MEAT LOAF

Magdalene Fiske, La Farge, Wisconsin
(PICTURED AT RIGHT)

If your taste buds call for pot roast but your pocketbook insists on ground beef—or you don't happen to have a roast on hand—here's the perfect solution! The vegetables take on the beefy goodness of the meat loaf's drippings—and save on cleanup, too, since they cook in the same dish.

        1 can (5 ounces) evaporated milk
    1/4 cup ketchup
    1/2 cup cracker crumbs
        2 tablespoons Worcestershire sauce
    1/2 teaspoon salt
    1/4 teaspoon pepper
        2 pounds lean ground beef
        4 small onions, quartered
        4 small potatoes, peeled and quartered
        4 medium carrots, quartered
        1 large green pepper, cut into strips
        2 tablespoons chopped fresh parsley

In a large bowl, combine milk, ketchup, cracker crumbs, Worcestershire sauce, salt and pepper. Add ground beef; mix well. Shape meat mixture into an 8-1/2-in. x 4-1/2-in. x 2-1/2-in. loaf and place in a 13-in. x 9-in. x 2-in. baking dish. Place onions, potatoes, carrots and green pepper around the loaf. Cover dish with foil. Bake

at 350° for 1-1/2 hours or until no pink remains in meat loaf and vegetables are tender. *Uncover for last 15 minutes of baking.* Sprinkle vegetables with parsley before serving. **Yield:** 6-8 servings.

CRISSCROSS MEAT LOAF

Betty Fugate, Plainfield, Indiana
(PICTURED AT RIGHT)

I found this recipe years ago, and keep coming back to it often…it's the meat loaf my family requests most!

        1 egg, beaten
    1/4 cup ketchup
        4 saltine crackers, crushed
        1 small onion, finely chopped
        1 tablespoon Worcestershire sauce
        1 teaspoon salt
    1/4 teaspoon ground thyme
    1/8 teaspoon pepper
    1-1/2 pounds lean ground beef
        2 to 3 ounces sliced American cheese

In a large bowl, combine egg, ketchup, crushed crackers, onion, Worcestershire sauce, salt, thyme and pepper. Add ground beef; mix well. In a shallow baking dish, shape meat mixture into a 7-in. x 3-in. x 2-in. loaf. Bake at 350° for 1 hour or until no pink remains. Cut cheese slices into strips; arrange strips in a crisscross pattern over meat loaf. Let stand a few minutes before serving. **Yield:** 6-8 servings.

MEXICAN MEAT LOAF ROLL

Vonnie White, Rapid City, South Dakota

If you've never made a "filled" meat loaf before, try this one first. It has a unique taste that folks of all ages take to—and when you serve it already sliced on a platter, it's really pretty, too!

        2 eggs, beaten
    1/4 cup quick-cooking *or* rolled oats
        1 tablespoon Worcestershire sauce
        1 teaspoon pepper
    1-1/2 pounds lean ground beef
        1 package (8 ounces) cream cheese, softened
        1 can (4 ounces) chopped green chilies, drained
    3/4 cup salsa

In a large bowl, combine eggs, oats, Worcestershire sauce and pepper. Add ground beef and mix well. On a piece of waxed paper, pat meat mixture into an 18-in. x 9-in. rectangle. Combine cream cheese and chilies; spread over meat to within 1 in. of outer edges. Roll meat mixture, jelly-roll style, starting at narrow end. Place seam side down in a 12-in. x 8-in. baking dish. Bake at 350° for 50 minutes. Drain excess fat. Top with salsa and bake another 10-15 minutes. Let stand 10 minutes before serving. **Yield:** 6-8 servings.

> **MEAT LOAF MAGIC.** Pictured at right from top to bottom: Carrot Meat Loaf, Pot Roast Meat Loaf and Crisscross Meat Loaf (all recipes on this page).

Meat-and-Potato Patties

Gladys Klein, Burlington, Wisconsin

During World War II, when meat was rationed and had to be purchased with tokens, this recipe went a long way in feeding a family. To this day, I still reach for it whenever I want something different from regular hamburgers. By the way, children really like these (just as I did when I was a child!).

  3/4 pound lean ground beef
  3/4 cup coarsely ground potatoes
  1/4 cup finely chopped onion
    2 tablespoons chopped green pepper
    1 egg, beaten
  1/4 teaspoon salt
    1 tablespoon cooking oil
    1 cup tomato juice
    1 tablespoon all-purpose flour
  1/4 cup water

In a large mixing bowl, combine beef, potatoes, onion, green pepper, egg and salt. Shape into four flat patties. Heat oil in a skillet. Brown the patties on both sides; drain. Add tomato juice. Simmer 20-25 minutes or until meat is no longer pink. Remove patties to a serving platter; keep warm. Combine flour and water; gradually add to juice in the skillet. Cook over medium-low heat, stirring constantly until thickened. Spoon over patties. Serve immediately. **Yield:** 4 servings.

Tomato-Rice Meatballs

Phyllis Miller, Hunta, Ontario

These individual round loaves are tasty with your favorite potatoes on the side...but they're even better (and more fun) when served as giant meatballs on top of spaghetti!

    4 slices bread, torn into small pieces
  1/2 cup milk
    1 egg, beaten
    1 pound lean ground beef
    2 celery stalks, chopped
  1/4 cup chopped onion
  1/4 cup uncooked instant rice
    1 teaspoon salt
  1/4 teaspoon pepper
    2 cups tomato sauce

In a large bowl, soak bread in milk. Add egg, ground beef, celery, onion, rice, salt and pepper. Mix well. Shape mixture into eight balls and place in a greased 2-1/2-qt. casserole. Pour tomato sauce over meatballs. Bake at 350° for 1-1/2 hours. **Yield:** 6-8 servings.

Stuffed Meat Loaf

Lisa Williams, Steamboat Springs, Colorado

My husband's job takes him away from home a good deal. When he returns, his first request is always for this stuffed meat loaf!

1-1/4 pounds lean ground beef
    1 pound bulk hot sausage

1-1/2 cups herb-seasoned dry bread stuffing
    1 egg, beaten
    5 tablespoons ketchup, *divided*
    3 tablespoons steak sauce, *divided*
    1 cup (4 ounces) shredded cheddar cheese
    1 small tomato, diced
    1 small onion, diced
  1/2 small green pepper, diced
    8 to 10 fresh mushrooms, sliced
    4 ounces thinly sliced fully cooked ham, optional
    1 cup (4 ounces) shredded Swiss cheese

In a mixing bowl, combine ground beef, sausage, stuffing, egg, 3 tablespoons ketchup and 2 tablespoons steak sauce. Mix well. Pat half of the meat mixture into a 9-in. x 5-in. x 2-in. loaf pan. Sprinkle with cheddar cheese. Layer with tomato, onion, green pepper, mushrooms, ham if desired and Swiss cheese. Cover with remaining meat mixture; press down firmly to seal. (Mixture may be higher than the top of the pan.) Combine remaining ketchup and steak sauce; drizzle over top of meat loaf. Bake at 350° for 1 hour or until no pink remains, draining off fat when necessary. **Yield:** 6-8 servings.

Busy-Day Meat Loaf

Carolina Hofeldt, Lloyd, Montana

When I'm busy working outside on our ranch (and I usually am!), there's nothing better than coming into the house and having my meal cooked to perfection while I'm gone from the kitchen. Here's a no-fuss, delicious meat loaf for those times when "the cook's not in". You don't even thaw the beef first!

    2 pounds lean ground beef
    1 can (10-3/4 ounces) condensed tomato soup, undiluted
    1 can (10-3/4 ounces) condensed mushroom soup, undiluted
    1 envelope (1 ounce) dry onion soup mix

Shape beef into a loaf and freeze. Place frozen loaf in a large piece of foil. Pour soups and dry soup mix over it; seal tightly. Place in pan. Bake at 300° for 4 hours. **Yield:** 6-8 servings.

Depression Meat Loaf

Violet Heaton, Portland, Oregon

This recipe really does date back to the 1930's. The secret to its "just-right" texture? It's all in the mixing process. You won't believe that such a grand meat loaf can be created from so few humble ingredients...until you try it for yourself!

  1/2 cup evaporated milk
    2 slices bread
  1/4 cup chopped onion
  3/4 teaspoon salt
  1/4 teaspoon pepper
    1 pound lean ground beef

In a large bowl, pour milk over bread. Let stand until the milk is absorbed. Add onion, salt and pepper. Stir with fork until bread softens and is light and fluffy. Mix in ground beef. In a shallow baking dish, shape into a 7-in. x 3-in. x 2-in. loaf. Bake at 350° for 50 minutes or until no pink remains. **Yield:** 4 servings.

—————— ▪ ▪ ▪ ——————

MOZZARELLA MEAT WHIRL
John Dailey, Rocky Mount, North Carolina

I've loved to cook for as long as I can remember. This recipe, which dates back to 1960, is an example of the special touches that I like to add to my dishes.

   1 pound lean ground beef
  1/4 pound ground pork
  1/4 pound ground veal
  1/2 cup dry bread crumbs
   1 egg, beaten
   1 tablespoon prepared mustard
   1 teaspoon salt
  1/8 teaspoon pepper
   2 cups (8 ounces) shredded mozzarella cheese
  1/4 cup chopped fresh parsley
SAUCE:
  3/4 cup ketchup
  1/2 cup water
   1 tablespoon Worcestershire sauce

In a large mixing bowl, combine beef, pork and veal; mix well. Add bread crumbs, egg, mustard, salt and pepper; blend well. On waxed paper, pat meat mixture into a 14-in. x 8-in. rectangle. Cover with mozzarella cheese and sprinkle with parsley. Starting at the narrow end, roll up tightly, jelly-roll style. Press ends firmly to seal. Place seam side down in a 9-in. x 5-in. x 2-1/2-in. loaf pan. For sauce, combine ketchup, water and Worcestershire sauce; pour over meat loaf. Bake at 350° for 1-1/4 hours or until no pink remains, basting frequently. **Yield:** 6 servings.

—————— ▪ ▪ ▪ ——————

MEAT LOAVES WITH PESTO SAUCE
Lou Ganser, Grafton, Wisconsin

The pesto sauce adds an herb and cheese flavor that makes this recipe unique. If you're a family of two, prepare the whole recipe and use the leftovers for sandwiches.

PESTO SAUCE:
   2 cups fresh spinach *or* parsley
   2 garlic cloves
  1/2 cup walnuts
   1 cup olive oil
   1 tablespoon dried basil
  1/2 cup grated Parmesan cheese
Salt and pepper to taste
MEAT LOAVES:
   1 pound lean ground beef
  1/2 teaspoon salt
  1/4 teaspoon pepper
  1/2 cup seasoned dry bread crumbs
  1/4 cup minced onion
   1 can (8 ounces) tomato sauce, *divided*
   1 egg, beaten
   1 tablespoon cooking oil
  1/4 cup water

Combine pesto ingredients in a blender or food processor. Cover and process until a smooth paste forms. Set aside. In a mixing bowl, combine ground beef, salt, pepper, bread crumbs, onion, 2 tablespoons tomato sauce, egg and 3 tablespoons pesto sauce; mix well. Shape into four loaves. In a skillet, heat oil. Brown meat loaves on all sides. Combine 1 tablespoon pesto sauce, remaining tomato sauce and water; pour over meat. Simmer, covered, for 20 minutes or until meat is no longer pink. Serve the loaves topped with tomato-pesto sauce. Refrigerate or freeze remaining pesto sauce for later use. **Yield:** 4 servings.

—————— ▪ ▪ ▪ ——————

MINI MEAT LOAVES
Judy Good, Charlotte, Michigan

My church group serves dinner to a business women's group once a month, so we're always on the lookout for new, exciting dishes like this one. It's fun to serve and have your guests guess what the ingredients are!

   3 eggs, beaten
  1/2 cup water *or* milk
   1 envelope (1 ounce) dry onion soup mix
1-1/2 cups soft bread crumbs
   3 pounds lean ground beef
SAUCE:
  3/4 cup bottled chili sauce
  3/4 cup water
  1/4 cup packed brown sugar
   1 can (16 ounces) sauerkraut, drained and snipped
   1 can (8 ounces) cranberry sauce

In a mixing bowl, combine eggs, water or milk, soup mix and bread crumbs. Add beef; mix well. Shape into 10 individual meat loaves about 4-in. x 2-1/2-in. each. Place in a 13-in. x 9-in. x 2-in. baking dish. Combine sauce ingredients; pour over meat loaves. Bake uncovered at 350° for 45 minutes or until no pink remains, basting once or twice with sauce. **Yield:** 10 servings.

—————— ▪ ▪ ▪ ——————

CLASSIC MEAT LOAF
Mary Rea, Orangeville, Ontario

It's not fancy, and it doesn't use exotic ingredients…but this is quite simply the best old-fashioned meat loaf I've ever made.

  1/2 cup milk
   3 slices whole wheat *or* white bread, cubed
   1 egg, beaten
   1 medium onion, chopped
   2 tablespoons chili sauce
   2 teaspoons Worcestershire sauce
   1 teaspoon salt
  1/2 teaspoon pepper
   2 to 5 drops hot pepper sauce
   2 pounds lean ground beef

In a large bowl, pour milk over bread. Add egg, onion, chili sauce, Worcestershire sauce, salt, pepper and hot pepper sauce; mix thoroughly. Add ground beef; mix well. Shape meat mixture into an 8-1/2-in. x 4-1/2-in. loaf. Bake in a shallow pan at 350° for 1-1/4 hours or until no pink remains. Drain. **Yield:** 8-10 servings.

Oven Meals

MEAT 'N' PEPPER CORN BREAD

Rita Carlson, Idaho Falls, Idaho
(PICTURED AT LEFT)

It suits me to be able to brown and bake this corn bread in the same cast-iron skillet—such convenience!

        1 pound ground beef
        1 cup chopped green pepper
        1 cup chopped onion
        2 cans (8 ounces *each*) tomato sauce
    1-1/2 teaspoons chili powder
      1/2 teaspoon salt
      1/4 teaspoon pepper
        1 cup all-purpose flour
      3/4 cup cornmeal
      1/4 cup sugar
        1 tablespoon baking powder
      1/2 teaspoon salt
        1 egg, beaten
        1 cup milk
      1/4 cup vegetable oil

In a 10-in. cast-iron skillet, lightly brown ground beef, green pepper and onion; drain. Add tomato sauce, chili powder, salt and pepper; simmer 10-15 minutes. Meanwhile, combine dry ingredients. Combine egg, milk and oil; stir into dry ingredients just until moistened. Pour over beef mixture. Bake at 400° for 25-30 minutes or until golden. Run knife around edge of skillet and invert on serving plate. Cut into wedges to serve. **Yield:** 4-6 servings.

MEAT-AND-POTATO CASSEROLE

Marna Heitz, Farley, Iowa
(PICTURED AT LEFT)

For variety, you can use another kind of cream soup (cream of mushroom, for instance). But try it this way first!

        3 to 4 cups thinly sliced peeled potatoes
        2 tablespoons butter *or* margarine, melted
      1/2 teaspoon salt
        1 pound ground beef
        1 package (10 ounces) frozen corn, thawed
        1 can (10-3/4 ounces) condensed cream
            of celery soup, undiluted
      1/3 cup milk
      1/4 teaspoon garlic powder
      1/8 teaspoon pepper
        1 tablespoon chopped onion

> **OLD-FASHIONED FAVORITES.** Pictured at left, clockwise from bottom: Salisbury Steak with Mushroom Sauce, Meat 'n' Pepper Corn Bread and Meat-and-Potato Casserole (recipes on this page).

        1 cup (4 ounces) shredded cheddar cheese,
            divided
Snipped fresh parsley, optional

Toss potatoes with butter and salt; arrange on the bottom and up the sides of a greased 12-in. x 8-in. x 2-in. casserole. Bake, uncovered, at 400° for 25-30 minutes or until potatoes are almost tender. Meanwhile, in a skillet, brown beef; drain. Sprinkle beef and corn over potatoes. Combine soup, milk, garlic powder, pepper, onion and 1/2 cup cheese; pour over beef mixture. Bake at 400°, uncovered, for 20 minutes or until vegetables are tender. Remove from oven; top with remaining cheese. Return to oven for 2-3 minutes or until the cheese is melted. Garnish with parsley if desired. **Yield:** 6 servings.

SALISBURY STEAK WITH MUSHROOM SAUCE

Mary Beth Jung, Grafton, Wisconsin
(PICTURED AT LEFT)

There are lots of Salisbury Steak recipes…but of all the ones I've tried, this is my all-time favorite—and my husband's, too!

MUSHROOM SAUCE:
        1 tablespoon dehydrated minced onion
        3 tablespoons butter *or* margarine
        3 tablespoons all-purpose flour
      1/8 teaspoon pepper
        1 can (4 ounces) mushrooms, liquid drained
            and reserved
        1 beef bouillon cube
Water
      1/4 teaspoon bottled browning sauce
SALISBURY STEAKS MIXTURE:
      1/3 cup minced onion
      1/3 cup minced green pepper
      1/4 cup chopped celery
        1 garlic clove, minced
        2 tablespoons butter *or* margarine
    1-1/2 pounds ground beef
        2 tablespoons minced chives *or* green
            onion tops
      1/2 teaspoon dry mustard
Dash paprika
        1 teaspoon salt
      1/2 teaspoon pepper

For sauce, in a small saucepan, melt butter and saute onion until soft. Stir in flour and pepper; blend well. Add mushrooms and bouillon. Add reserved mushroom liquid and enough water to make 1-1/4 cups; stir and cook until thickened. Stir in browning sauce. Keep warm while preparing the Salisbury steaks. In a skillet, saute onion, green pepper, celery and garlic in butter over low heat. Remove from heat and add to remaining ingredients; mix well. Shape into six patties, about 3/4 in. thick. Place on a broiler rack. Broil about 7 minutes; turn and broil about 5 minutes longer or until cooked through. Serve with Mushroom Sauce. **Yield:** 6 servings.

■ ■ ■

SALISBURY SAUERBRATEN
Lillian DePauw, Newark, New York

I've been making this for at least 20 years. It combines the tastes of two of my favorite meat dishes.

- 1 can (10-1/2 ounces) beef gravy, *divided*
- 1 pound lean ground beef
- 1/3 cup dry bread crumbs
- 1 tablespoon minced onion
- 1/4 teaspoon grated lemon peel
- 1/2 teaspoon ground ginger
- 1 can (16 ounces) small whole new potatoes, drained
- 1/4 cup finely crushed gingersnaps
- 1 tablespoon brown sugar
- 2 tablespoons red wine vinegar

In a mixing bowl, combine 1/3 cup gravy, ground beef, bread crumbs, onion, lemon peel and ginger. Mix thoroughly. Shape into four loaves. Place in an 11-in. x 7-in. x 1-1/2-in. baking dish. Bake at 350°, uncovered, for 20 minutes. Remove from oven and spoon off excess fat. Arrange potatoes around loaves. Combine remaining gravy with gingersnaps, brown sugar and vinegar. Pour over meat and potatoes. Cover and bake an additional 25-35 minutes or until hot and bubbly. **Yield:** 4 servings.

■ ■ ■

CANNELLONI
Susan Longyear, Washington, Virginia

Two sauces make this satisfying dish doubly delicious!

FILLING:
- 1 large onion, finely chopped
- 1 garlic clove, minced
- 2 tablespoons olive oil
- 1 package (10 ounces) frozen chopped spinach, thawed and squeezed dry
- 1 pound ground beef
- 1/4 cup grated Parmesan cheese
- 2 tablespoons heavy cream
- 2 eggs, lightly beaten
- 1/2 teaspoon dried oregano
- 1 teaspoon salt
- 1/4 teaspoon pepper
- 10 lasagna noodles
- 1 can (24 ounces) tomato sauce, *divided*

CREAM SAUCE:
- 6 tablespoons butter *or* margarine
- 6 tablespoons all-purpose flour
- 1 cup milk
- 1 cup heavy cream

Salt and pepper to taste
- 1/2 cup grated Parmesan cheese

Saute onion and garlic in olive oil until soft. Stir in spinach. Cook, stirring constantly, about 5 minutes or until all the water has evaporated and the spinach starts to stick to the pan. Turn into a large mixing bowl. Brown meat; drain and add to spinach mixture. Add Parmesan cheese, cream, eggs, oregano, salt and pepper; mix well. Set aside. Cook lasagna noodles accord-

ing to package directions; drain. Cut each noodle in half crosswise; spread out noodles side by side on a large piece of foil. Place 1 heaping tablespoon of filling at one end of noodle; roll up. Repeat with remaining noodles and filling. To assemble, pour about 1 cup of tomato sauce into the bottom of a 13-in. x 9-in. x 2-in. baking dish. Place two rolls, seam side down, vertically on both sides of the baking dish. Place remaining rolls in four rows of three rolls each; set aside. For cream sauce, melt butter in a heavy saucepan over medium heat. Remove from heat; stir in flour. Return to heat; add milk and cream all at once. Stirring constantly, cook over medium heat until well blended. Bring to a boil, reduce heat and simmer, stirring constantly, about 1 minute longer or until the sauce is thick enough to coat the spoon. Remove from heat; season with salt and pepper. Spread cream sauce over lasagne rolls. Cover with remaining tomato sauce. Sprinkle with Parmesan cheese. Bake at 375°, uncovered, for 20-30 minutes or until hot and bubbly. **Yield:** 8-10 servings.

■ ■ ■

JUMBLE LALA
Dora Brahmer, Spring Valley, Wisconsin

Wondering about the silly name? It came about because this dish has all the spicy goodness of jambalaya—but requires a lot less time and work to prepare!

- 1-1/2 pounds ground beef, browned and drained
- 1 medium onion, chopped
- 1 quart tomato juice
- 1 can (10-3/4 ounces) condensed tomato soup, undiluted
- 1 cup uncooked long grain rice
- 1 tablespoon brown sugar
- 1/4 teaspoon dried thyme
- 2 bay leaves
- 1/4 to 1/2 teaspoon curry powder
- 1 teaspoon salt
- 1/2 teaspoon pepper

Combine all ingredients in a large mixing bowl. Pour into a greased 2-qt. casserole dish. Cover and bake at 350° for 80-90 minutes or until hot and bubbly. **Yield:** 8-10 servings.

■ ■ ■

CORN BREAD WITH BLACK-EYED PEAS
Jeanne Shinn, Bandera, Texas

Black-eyed peas are a good-luck tradition for New Year's Day...but my family is so fond of this recipe, I make it all year long!

- 1 pound ground beef, browned and drained
- 1 cup cornmeal
- 1/2 cup all-purpose flour
- 3/4 cup cream-style corn
- 1 cup cooked *or* canned black-eyed peas, drained
- 1 medium onion, chopped
- 1/2 cup vegetable oil
- 1 cup buttermilk

2 eggs, beaten
2 cups (8 ounces) shredded cheddar cheese
1/2 teaspoon baking soda

In a mixing bowl, combine all ingredients and mix well. Pour into a greased 13-in. x 9-in. x 2-in. baking dish. Bake at 350°, uncovered, for 40-45 minutes or until bread is golden. **Yield:** 8-10 servings.

HOBO KNAPSACKS

Ann Millhouse, Polo, Illinois

When our children were small, I invented this recipe to take along on trips to the park. We'd grill the packets, then eat the meal right from the foil wrap!

2 medium potatoes, peeled and thinly sliced
2 large tomatoes, chopped
1 large onion, chopped
1 package (10 ounces) frozen mixed
   vegetables, thawed
1 can (4 ounces) mushrooms, drained
1 pound lean ground beef
1/2 cup tomato juice
1/2 cup rolled oats
1 egg, beaten
1 tablespoon minced onion
1 teaspoon salt
1/4 teaspoon pepper
6 sheets heavy-duty aluminum foil
   (18 inches x 12 inches)
Additional salt and pepper, optional

In a mixing bowl, combine potatoes, tomatoes, onion, mixed vegetables and mushrooms; set aside. In another bowl, combine ground beef, tomato juice, oats, egg, onion, salt and pepper; mix well. Divide mixture into six portions; crumble each portion onto a piece of foil. Spoon the vegetable mixture over beef mixture. Season with additional salt and pepper if desired. Tightly fold up the foil around the beef and vegetables to form a pouch. Bake at 350° for 50-60 minutes or until the meat is cooked and the potatoes are tender. **Yield:** 6 servings.

CHEESE 'N' PASTA IN A POT

Carmelita Guinan, Wollaston, Massachusetts

I love to make this dish whenever friends are visiting. Since I can make it ahead, it gives me more time to spend with my guests. Warm rolls and a simple salad make this a meal.

2 pounds ground beef
1 large onion, chopped
1 garlic clove, minced
1 jar (14 ounces) spaghetti sauce
1 can (14-1/2 ounces) stewed tomatoes
1 can (4 ounces) mushroom stems and pieces,
   drained
8 ounces shell macaroni
2 cups (16 ounces) sour cream, *divided*
6 ounces sliced provolone cheese
6 ounces sliced mozzarella cheese

In a large skillet, brown ground beef with onion and garlic; drain. Stir in spaghetti sauce, stewed tomatoes

and mushrooms. Simmer for 20 minutes, uncovered. Meanwhile, cook macaroni according to package directions; drain and rinse with cold water. Spoon half of the shells into a Dutch oven or 4-qt. casserole. Layer with half of the meat mixture. Spread 1 cup of sour cream over meat sauce. Cover with provolone cheese. Repeat layers with remaining ingredients, ending with mozzarella cheese. Cover and bake at 350° for 30-40 minutes or until bubbly and heated through. **Yield:** 8-10 servings.

POTATO PIZZA HOT DISH

Diane VandeZande, Fountain, Minnesota

Even the pickiest eaters will dig right in when this is on the supper menu!

3 to 4 cups sliced peeled potatoes
1 can (11 ounces) condensed cheddar
   cheese soup, undiluted
1/2 cup milk
1-1/2 pounds ground beef
1 medium onion, chopped
1 jar (14 ounces) pizza sauce
2 cups (8 ounces) shredded mozzarella cheese

Cover bottom of a greased 13-in. x 9-in. x 2-in. baking dish with potatoes. Combine soup and milk; pour over potatoes. In a skillet, brown ground beef with onion; drain. Spread over soup mixture. Pour pizza sauce over meat layer. Cover and bake at 350° for 80-90 minutes or until the potatoes are tender. Sprinkle with cheese; return to oven until cheese is melted, about 5 minutes. **Yield:** 8 servings.

SKILLET CASSEROLE

Joan Govier, Victoria Harbour, Ontario

If my family and friends gave out blue ribbons for their favorite casserole dish, this casserole would win a fistful!

1 green pepper, diced
2 medium onions, diced
1 tablespoon butter *or* margarine
1 pound ground beef
2 medium tomatoes, seeded and chopped
4 medium potatoes, peeled, cut into
   1/2-inch cubes and parboiled
1/4 cup chili sauce
1 can (10-3/4 ounces) cream of chicken
   soup, undiluted
3/4 teaspoon salt
1/4 teaspoon pepper
1/4 cup grated Parmesan cheese

In a skillet, cook green pepper and onions in butter until tender. Remove and set aside. In the same skillet, brown ground beef; drain. Add green peppers, onion, tomatoes and potatoes. Stir in chili sauce and soup; mix well. Pour into a greased 13-in. x 9-in. x 2-in. baking dish. Sprinkle with salt, pepper and Parmesan cheese. Bake at 350°, uncovered, for 15 minutes or until lightly browned and bubbly. **Yield:** 4 servings.

Beef-Stuffed Acorn Squash

Jean Gaines, Bullhead City, Arizona

(PICTURED AT LEFT)

My husband is retired, so we do quite a bit of traveling. I like to cook, travel and add to my collection of fund-raiser cookbooks. I have one from every state except Vermont!

2 small acorn squash, halved and seeded
1/2 cup water
1/2 pound ground beef
2 tablespoons chopped onion
2 tablespoons chopped celery
2 tablespoons all-purpose flour
1/2 teaspoon salt
1/2 teaspoon ground sage
3/4 cup milk
1/2 cup cooked rice
1/4 cup shredded cheddar cheese

Invert squash in an 11-in. x 7-in. x 1-1/2-in. baking dish. Add water and cover with foil. Bake at 375° for 50-60 minutes or until tender. Meanwhile, brown ground beef with onion and celery; drain. Stir in flour, salt and sage. Add milk, stirring until thickened and bubbly. Stir in rice. Transfer squash to a baking sheet. Fill cavity with meat mixture. Bake at 350° for 30 minutes. Remove from oven; sprinkle with cheese and bake 3-5 minutes longer or until cheese is melted. **Yield:** 4 servings.

Midwest Meatball Casserole

Judy Larson, Greendale, Wisconsin

(PICTURED AT LEFT)

I've relied on this recipe many times as a soothing finish to a hectic day...and since I usually have all the ingredients on hand, there's no last-minute rush to the store, either.

2 cans (8 ounces *each*) tomato sauce, *divided*
1 pound lean ground beef
1 egg
1/4 cup dry bread crumbs
1/4 cup chopped onion
1 teaspoon salt
1 package (10 ounces) frozen mixed vegetables
1/2 teaspoon dried thyme
1/8 teaspoon pepper
1 package (16 ounces) frozen hash brown potatoes, thawed
1 tablespoon butter *or* margarine, melted
3 ounces American cheese slices, cut into 1/2-inch strips

In a mixing bowl, combine 2 tablespoons tomato sauce with beef, egg, bread crumbs, onion and salt. Shape into 1-in. balls. Place on a jelly roll pan and bake at 375° for 15-20 minutes or until the meatballs are browned. Meanwhile, in a skillet or large saucepan, combine remaining tomato sauce with vegetables and seasonings. Cover and simmer for 10-15 minutes or until heated through; stir in meatballs and set aside. Place potatoes in a greased 11-in. x 7-in. x 2-in. baking dish. Brush with butter and bake at 375° for 15-20 minutes or until lightly browned. Remove from oven; top with meatball mixture. Arrange cheese strips in a lattice pattern on top; return to oven for 20 minutes. **Yield:** 6 servings.

COMPANY'S COMING. Pictured at left, clockwise from bottom: Mock Filet Mignon, Beef-Stuffed Acorn Squash, Midwest Meatball Casserole (recipes above).

Mock Filet Mignon

Cheri Legaard, Fortuna, North Dakota

(PICTURED AT LEFT)

I get rave reviews—and plenty of requests for the recipe!—whenever I serve this to friends and family.

1-1/2 pounds lean ground beef
2 cups cooked rice
1 cup minced onion
1/4 teaspoon garlic powder
1 tablespoon Worcestershire sauce
1-1/2 teaspoons salt
1/4 teaspoon pepper
6 bacon strips

In a mixing bowl, combine ground beef, rice, onion, garlic powder, Worcestershire sauce, salt and pepper. Mix thoroughly. Shape into six round patties. Wrap a strip of bacon around each patty; fasten with a wooden toothpick. Place in an ungreased shallow baking dish. Bake at 450° for 20 minutes or to desired doneness. **Yield:** 6 servings.

Zucchini Garden Casserole

Dordana Mason, Iowa City, Iowa

Zucchini is best picked when it's small and tender. Store it in your shed or garage...or, when the weather is freezing, keep it in a cool room of your basement.

4 medium tomatoes, peeled and sliced
4 medium zucchini (about 1-1/2 pounds), sliced
2 teaspoons salt, *divided*
1-1/2 pounds lean ground beef
2/3 cup uncooked long grain rice
2 tablespoons chopped fresh parsley
1/4 cup chopped green pepper
1/4 cup chopped onion
1/4 teaspoon ground cinnamon
1/4 teaspoon ground allspice
1/4 teaspoon pepper
1 cup tomato juice
1 cup (4 ounces) shredded Colby cheese

Arrange half of the tomatoes in a greased 13-in. x 9-in. x 2-in. baking dish. Layer with half of the zucchini; sprinkle with 1/2 teaspoon salt. In a mixing bowl, combine ground beef, rice, parsley, green pepper, onion, spices, pepper and 1 teaspoon salt; mix well. Spoon over tomato layer. Cover with remaining zucchini and tomatoes. Sprinkle with remaining salt. Cover and bake at 375° for 1-1/2 hours. Uncover and sprinkle with cheese. Bake 15 minutes longer or until cheese melts. **Yield:** 6-8 servings.

■ ■ ■

CAMPFIRE BEANS
Flo Rahn, Hillsboro, Kansas
(PICTURED AT RIGHT)

Served with cheese-topped corn bread, this is delicious!

1/3 cup packed brown sugar
1/2 cup ketchup
1 teaspoon dry mustard
1/2 cup barbecue sauce
1/3 cup sugar
1/2 teaspoon chili powder
1/2 teaspoon salt
1/4 teaspoon pepper
1/2 pound ground beef, browned and drained
1/2 pound bacon, cooked, drained and crumbled
1/2 pound bratwurst, cut into 1-inch slices, cooked and drained
1 can (15 ounces) kidney beans, rinsed and drained
1 can (16 ounces) pork and beans
1 can (15 ounces) chili pinto beans in sauce
1 can (16 ounces) green lima beans, rinsed and drained

In a large mixing bowl, combine first eight ingredients; mix well. Add cooked beef, bacon and bratwurst. Stir in all of the beans. Pour into a 2-qt. casserole. Bake at 350°, uncovered, for 1 hour or until heated through. **Yield:** 10-12 servings.

■ ■ ■

ZESTY BEEF CORN BREAD DINNER
Edith Lawler, Clinton, Missouri
(PICTURED AT RIGHT)

These Southwestern-inspired squares are delicious by themselves, of course—but the sauce gives them an extra "zing" of zesty flavor, and I never make this recipe without it!

1 pound ground beef
1/3 chopped onion
1 garlic clove, minced
1/4 cup ketchup
1 teaspoon salt
1 box (8-1/2 ounces) corn muffin mix
1 cup (4 ounces) shredded cheddar cheese
TANGY TOMATO SAUCE:
2 tablespoons cold water
2 teaspoons cornstarch
1 can (8 ounces) tomatoes with juice, cut up
1/4 teaspoon chili powder
1/4 teaspoon ground cumin
1/4 teaspoon garlic powder
1 teaspoon sugar
2 tablespoons chopped chili peppers
2 tablespoons chopped green pepper
1 teaspoon Worcestershire sauce

In a skillet, brown beef, onion and garlic; drain. Stir in ketchup and salt. Prepare corn muffin mix according to package directions. Spread half of the batter into a greased 8-in. square baking dish. Spoon beef mixture over batter; sprinkle with cheese. Spread remaining batter over cheese. Bake at 350° for 30-35 minutes or until golden brown. Meanwhile, combine sauce ingredients in a small saucepan. Cook and stir over medium heat until thickened. Let bread stand for 5 minutes after removing from oven; cut into squares and spoon sauce over. **Yield:** 6-8 servings.

■ ■ ■

TATER-TOPPED CASSEROLE
Victoria Mitchell, Salem, Virginia
(PICTURED AT RIGHT)

I grew up enjoying this dish. My mother always saw smiles around the table whenever she served it!

1/2 cup chopped onion
1/3 cup sliced celery
1 pound lean ground beef
1/2 teaspoon salt
1/4 teaspoon pepper
1 can (10-3/4 ounces) condensed cream of celery soup, undiluted
1 package (16 ounces) frozen fried potato nuggets
1 cup (4 ounces) shredded cheddar cheese

In a skillet, cook onion, celery and ground beef until the meat is brown and the vegetables are tender. Drain. Stir in salt and pepper. Spoon mixture into a greased 12-in. x 8-in. x 2-in. baking dish. Spread soup over meat mixture. Top with frozen potatoes. Bake at 400° about 40 minutes or until bubbly. Remove from oven and sprinkle with cheese. Return to oven and bake until cheese melts, about 5 minutes. **Yield:** 4-6 servings.

■ ■ ■

POOR MAN'S DINNER
Mila Abner, Vada, Kentucky

Don't let the name fool you—this dish guarantees "million-dollar taste" with just a few ingredients!

1 pound ground beef
1/4 teaspoon pepper
1/4 teaspoon garlic powder
5 large potatoes, peeled and sliced
1 large onion, sliced
2 cans (10-3/4 ounces *each*) condensed cream of mushroom soup, undiluted
Chopped fresh parsley

In a skillet, brown ground beef; drain. Season with pepper and garlic powder. In a 1-1/2-qt. casserole, thinly layer the beef, potatoes and onion slices. Pour soup over all. Cover and bake at 350° for 1 hour or until potatoes are tender. Garnish with parsley. **Yield:** 6 servings.

CHEESY BEEF DINNER: Substitute 2 cans (11 ounces *each*) condensed cheddar cheese soup, undiluted, for the mushroom soup.

RUSTIC ROUNDUP. Pictured at right, clockwise from bottom: Zesty Beef Corn Bread Dinner, Tater-Topped Casserole and Campfire Beans (recipes on this page).

■ ■ ■
BEEF AND POTATO CASSEROLE
Brenda Bradshaw, Oconto, Wisconsin

My husband goes to school and works full-time, and I'm the mother of a 1-year-old. With a busy schedule like ours, this quick recipe of pantry staples is just perfect!

 4 cups frozen potato rounds
 1 pound ground beef
 1 package (10 ounces) frozen chopped broccoli, thawed
 1 can (10-3/4 ounces) condensed cream of celery soup, undiluted
 1/3 cup milk
 1 cup (4 ounces) shredded cheddar cheese, *divided*
 1/4 teaspoon garlic powder
 1/8 teaspoon pepper

Place potato rounds on the bottom and up the sides of a 13-in. x 9-in. x 2-in. baking dish. Bake at 400° for 10 minutes. Meanwhile, brown beef; drain. Place beef and broccoli over potatoes. Combine celery soup, milk, 1/2 cup cheddar cheese, garlic powder and pepper. Pour over beef mixture. Cover and bake at 400° for 20 minutes. Top with remaining cheese. Return to oven for 2-3 minutes or until the cheese melts. **Yield:** 6 servings.

■ ■ ■
SAUERKRAUT-BEEF BAKE
Dolores Skrout, Summerhill, Pennsylvania

This dish travels well to a cookout—bake it, then transfer to one of those disposable aluminum pans. Place it on the back of the grill to keep warm while the meat is cooking. Sauerkraut always tastes good with hot dogs and other barbecued sandwiches.

 1 pound ground beef
 1 can (27 ounces) sauerkraut, undrained
 1/2 cup uncooked instant rice
 1 can (10-3/4 ounces) condensed cream of mushroom soup, undiluted
 1 soup can water
 1/2 package dry onion soup mix
 1 can (4 ounces) mushroom stems and pieces, drained, optional

In a skillet, brown ground beef. Drain. In a greased 2-qt. casserole, combine beef with sauerkraut, rice, soup, water and soup mix. Add mushrooms if desired. Cover and bake at 350° for 1 hour. Recipe can easily be doubled for a larger group. **Yield:** 6 servings.

■ ■ ■
MEATBALLS WITH RICE
Mina Dyck, Boissevain, Manitoba

A pound of ground beef goes a long way in this recipe. I especially like to take it to potluck suppers.

 1 pound ground beef
 1/2 cup rolled oats
 1-1/2 teaspoons salt, *divided*
 1/2 teaspoon pepper
 1/2 teaspoon celery salt
 1 teaspoon dried parsley flakes
 2 cans (10-3/4 ounces *each*) condensed cream of asparagus soup, undiluted
 2 cups water
 1 cup uncooked rice
 1-1/2 cups sliced celery
 1 large onion, chopped
 1 can (4 ounces) mushroom stems and pieces, undrained

In a mixing bowl, combine ground beef, oats, 1/2 teaspoon salt, pepper, celery salt and parsley. Shape by tablespoonfuls into meatballs; place on a greased baking sheet. Bake at 400° for 18-20 minutes or until browned. Meanwhile, combine rice, celery, onion, mushrooms, soup, water and remaining salt. Transfer meatballs to a greased 3-qt. casserole; pour soup mixture over. Cover and bake at 350° for 1 hour or until liquid is absorbed and rice is tender. **Yield:** 6-8 servings.

■ ■ ■
SHORTCUT LASAGNA
Jeannette Anderson, Lake Village, Indiana

My mother and I have been making this lasagna for more than 15 years. The "shortcut" is not having to cook the noodles first, so it's not only quick and easy, but also delicious. My husband and our three children all love it when we have this for dinner.

 1-1/2 pounds ground beef
 1 can (28 ounces) tomatoes with juice, cut up
 1 can (8 ounces) tomato sauce
 2 envelopes (1.5 ounces *each*) spaghetti sauce mix
 2 cans (12 ounces *each*) vegetable juice
 9 uncooked lasagna noodles
 1 carton (16 ounces) cottage cheese
 2 cups (8 ounces) shredded mozzarella cheese

In a skillet, brown ground beef; drain. Stir in tomatoes, tomato sauce, spaghetti sauce mix and vegetable juice. Bring to a boil; reduce heat and simmer for 10 minutes. Remove from the heat. Cover the bottom of a lightly greased 13-in. x 9-in. x 2-in. baking dish with a thin layer of meat sauce. On top of that, layer three lasagna noodles, one-third of the cottage cheese, one-third of the mozzarella cheese and one-third of the remaining meat sauce. Repeat layers twice. Cover tightly with foil and bake at 350° for 1 hour or until heated through. Let stand 10 minutes before cutting. **Yield:** 12 servings.

■ ■ ■
BEEF AND BROCCOLI CASSEROLE
Dorothy Buttrill, Fairfield, Texas

I came up with this recipe on one of those "what in the world can I fix for dinner" days. I usually have the ingredients in the freezer and pantry, so it's handy when I need to fix a meal in a hurry.

 1 pound ground beef
 1/2 cup chopped onion
 1 tablespoon olive *or* vegetable oil

1 tablespoon Worcestershire sauce
1 teaspoon garlic salt
1 teaspoon Italian seasoning
1 cup uncooked instant rice
1 can (10-3/4 ounces) condensed cream of mushroom soup, undiluted
1/2 cup water
2 pounds fresh broccoli, chopped *or* 2 packages (10 ounces *each*) frozen chopped broccoli, cooked and drained
6 ounces sliced mozzarella cheese
Chopped fresh parsley, optional

In a skillet, brown beef and onion in oil until beef is browned and onion is tender; drain. Combine beef with Worcestershire sauce, garlic salt, Italian seasoning, rice, soup and water. Place cooked broccoli in an 11-in. x 7-in. x 2-in. baking dish; spoon meat mixture over. Top with mozzarella cheese. Bake, uncovered, at 400° for 15-20 minutes. Garnish with parsley if desired. **Yield:** 6 servings.

■ ■ ■

HEARTLAND MEAT CAKES

Virginia Bloomenrader, Highmore, South Dakota

Meats representative of America's Heartland—beef, pork and ham—are all used in this recipe, which I inherited from my mother. It makes a filling meal and is one of our family's favorites.

1/2 pound lean ground beef
1/2 pound lean ground pork
1/2 pound ground smoked ham
1 egg
1 small onion, chopped
1 cup mashed potatoes
1-1/2 cups fine bread crumbs
1 cup milk
1/2 teaspoon salt
1/2 teaspoon pepper
1 can (10-3/4 ounces) condensed tomato soup, undiluted
1/2 cup water

In a mixing bowl, combine beef, pork, ham, egg, onion, mashed potatoes, bread crumbs, milk, salt and pepper; mix until thoroughly combined. Divide into 12 portions, about 1/2 cup each, and shape into oval cakes. Place 1 in. apart in a greased 13-in. x 9-in. x 2-in. baking dish. Combine soup and water; pour over meat. Cover with foil; bake at 350° for 45 minutes, basting occasionally. Uncover and bake an additional 10 minutes. **Yield:** 6 servings.

■ ■ ■

SAUERKRAUT HOT DISH

Lucy Mohlman, Crete, Nebraska

This dish was brought to our school picnic by a neighbor. She took home an empty pan—and we all took home the recipe!

1 pound ground beef
1/4 cup chopped onion
1/2 teaspoon salt

1/2 teaspoon pepper
1 can (32 ounces) sauerkraut, drained
2 cups uncooked egg noodles
1 can (10-3/4 ounces) condensed cream of celery soup, undiluted
1 can (10-3/4 ounces) condensed cream of mushroom soup, undiluted
1 cup milk
1 to 1-1/2 cups (4 to 6 ounces) shredded cheddar cheese

In a skillet, brown ground beef, onion, salt and pepper; drain. Spoon half of the ground beef mixture into a 13-in. x 9-in. x 2-in. baking dish. Top with half of the sauerkraut and half of the noodles. Repeat layers. Combine soups and milk; pour over noodles. Cover and bake at 350° for 30 minutes. Remove from oven and sprinkle with cheese; return to oven for 15-20 minutes. **Yield:** 4-6 servings.

■ ■ ■

TWO-SQUASH LASAGNA

Marilyn Stroud, Larsen, Wisconsin

I learned to cook when I was growing up on a dairy farm and was a member of 4-H. This is one of my favorite recipes...it makes good use of the abundance of squash we always seem to have in summer and fall. You'll also find it freezes and reheats well.

1 pound ground beef
1 small onion, chopped
1 can (27-1/2 ounces) spaghetti sauce
1/2 teaspoon fennel seed, crushed
1 teaspoon salt
1/2 teaspoon pepper
2 cups (8 ounces) shredded mozzarella cheese, *divided*
1 carton (16 ounces) small curd cottage cheese *or* ricotta cheese
2 eggs, beaten
2 medium zucchini, sliced lengthwise into 1/2-inch strips
4 tablespoons all-purpose flour
1 small unpeeled yellow squash, shredded
1/4 cup grated Parmesan cheese

In a skillet, brown ground beef with onion; drain. Stir in spaghetti sauce, fennel seed, salt and pepper; set aside. In a small bowl, combine 1 cup mozzarella cheese, cottage or ricotta cheese and eggs. Place half the zucchini in a greased 13-in. x 9-in. x 2-in. baking dish; sprinkle with half the flour. Top with half the meat sauce and half the cheese mixture. Repeat layers of zucchini, flour, meat sauce and cheese mixture. Combine remaining mozzarella with summer squash; spoon over cheese mixture. Sprinkle with Parmesan. Bake at 375° for 50 minutes or until zucchini is tender. Let stand 10 minutes before serving. **Yield:** 8-10 servings.

■ ■ ■

BEEF FLORENTINE
Cindy Waltner, Columbus, Montana

Even my three small children—who won't touch spinach in any other way—enjoy this meal!

      2 pounds ground beef
      1 medium onion, chopped
      1 garlic clove, minced
      1 package (10 ounces) frozen chopped spinach
      1 jar (14 ounces) spaghetti sauce
      1 can (6 ounces) tomato paste
      1 can (8 ounces) tomato sauce
      1 teaspoon salt
      1 teaspoon pepper
      7 ounces elbow macaroni, cooked and drained
      1 cup (4 ounces) shredded cheddar cheese
  1-1/2 cups soft bread crumbs
      2 eggs, beaten

In a large skillet, brown beef with onion and garlic; drain. Cook spinach according to package directions. Drain spinach, reserving cooking liquid; add enough water to make 1 cup. Set spinach aside. In a small bowl, combine cooking liquid, spaghetti sauce, tomato paste, tomato sauce, salt and pepper; mix well. Stir sauce into skillet and simmer for 10 minutes. In a large bowl, combine macaroni, cheese, bread crumbs, eggs and cooked spinach; mix well. Spread into a greased 13-in. x 9-in. x 2-in. baking dish. Cover with meat sauce. Bake at 350° for 30 minutes. Let stand 5 minutes before serving. **Yield:** 10-12 servings.

■ ■ ■

MEATBALLS IN POTATO CUPS
Bettye Jecmenek, Columbus, Texas

I make this often for company. The potato cups make a unique and edible "container" for the meatballs.

      2 cups leftover mashed potatoes
      1 egg
  1/2 small onion, finely chopped
      1 celery stalk, finely chopped
  2/3 pound lean ground beef
  1/2 cup quick-cooking oats
  1/3 cup nonfat dry milk
  1/2 teaspoon salt
  1/4 teaspoon pepper
BOUILLON GRAVY:
      1 tablespoon butter *or* margarine
      2 tablespoons all-purpose flour
      1 cup water
      1 teaspoon beef bouillon granules
  1/2 teaspoon bottled browning sauce,
        optional

In a mixing bowl, combine potatoes and egg. Using an ice cream scoop, place eight mounds of potato mixture onto a greased jelly roll pan. Combine onion, celery, beef, oats, milk, salt and pepper; shape into eight meatballs. Press one meatball halfway into each potato "cup". Bake at 350° for 35-40 minutes or until the meat and potatoes are browned. Meanwhile, for gravy,

melt butter in a small saucepan; remove from the heat. Blend in flour. Stir in water and bouillon. Add browning sauce if desired. Cook and stir until smooth and thickened. Spoon gravy over potato cups and pass any remaining gravy. **Yield:** 4 servings.

■ ■ ■

CRUNCHY BEEF BAKE
Janie Moore, Marion, Ohio

I always use corkscrew noodles when preparing this, because the sauce seems to cling to them better than it does to flat noodles—ensuring plenty of good taste in every bite!

      2 cups corkscrew noodles
      1 pound ground beef
  3/4 cup chopped green pepper
      1 garlic clove, minced
      1 can (10-3/4 ounces) condensed cream
        of mushroom soup, undiluted
      1 can (14-1/2 ounces) tomatoes with
        liquid, cut up
  3/4 cup shredded cheddar cheese
  3/4 teaspoon seasoned salt
      1 can (2.8 ounces) french-fried onions

Cook noodles as directed on package. Meanwhile, brown ground beef with green pepper and garlic until beef is browned and green pepper is tender; drain. Drain noodles; combine with beef mixture, soup, tomatoes, cheese and salt. Spoon into a greased 2-qt. casserole. Cover and bake at 350° for 30-40 minutes. Uncover; top with french-fried onions and bake 5 minutes longer. **Yield:** 4-6 servings.

■ ■ ■

COMPANY CASSEROLE
Edna Davis, Denver, Colorado

Don't wait for "company" to serve this—it's delicious anytime. I found the recipe many years ago in a cookbook sponsored by a local radio program.

      2 pounds lean ground beef
  1/2 cup sour cream
      3 tablespoons dry onion soup mix
      1 egg, beaten
  1-1/2 cups soft bread crumbs
  1/4 cup butter *or* margarine
      1 can (8 ounces) mushroom stems and pieces
        with liquid
      1 can (10-3/4 ounces) condensed cream
        of chicken soup, undiluted
  1-2/3 cups water
SAUCE: (optional)
      1 can (10-3/4 ounces) condensed cream
        of chicken soup, undiluted
  1/4 teaspoon poultry seasoning
      1 teaspoon dried minced onion
  1/2 cup sour cream
BUTTER CRUMB DUMPLINGS:
      2 cups all-purpose flour
      4 teaspoons baking powder
      1 tablespoon poppy seed
      1 teaspoon celery salt

1 teaspoon poultry seasoning
2 teaspoons dried minced onion
1/4 cup vegetable oil
3/4 cup plus 2 tablespoons milk
1/4 cup butter *or* margarine, melted
2 cups soft bread crumbs

In a mixing bowl, combine first five ingredients. Shape into 16 balls. Melt butter in a skillet; brown meatballs over medium-low heat. Stir in mushrooms, soup and water. Simmer 20 minutes, adding more water if necessary. Turn into a 3-qt. casserole. If extra sauce is desired, combine cream of chicken soup, poultry seasoning and minced onion in a small saucepan. Cook until heated through. Remove from heat and stir in sour cream; pour over meatball mixture. For dumplings, combine flour, baking powder, poppy seed, celery salt, poultry seasoning and onion in a mixing bowl. Stir in oil and milk. Combine butter and bread crumbs. Drop heaping tablespoonsful of dough into buttered crumbs; roll to coat evenly. Cover meatball mixture with dumplings. Bake at 400°, uncovered, for 20-25 minutes or until dumplings are golden. **Yield:** 4-6 servings.

HAMBURGER RICE HOT DISH

Jan Franks, Oelwein, Iowa

What could be simpler than this supper? Not much! I round out this meal with steamed mixed vegetables and whatever fresh fruit is handy.

1 pound ground beef
1 can (10-3/4 ounces) condensed cream of chicken soup, undiluted
1 cup water
1 cup uncooked instant rice
Fresh chopped parsley

In a skillet, brown ground beef; drain. Add remaining ingredients; stir to combine. Spoon into a 1-1/2-qt. casserole dish. Cover and bake at 325° for 50-60 minutes. **Yield:** 4-6 servings.

BEEF AND MASHED POTATO CASSEROLE

Debra Hufsey, Newland, North Carolina

The tomato bisque soup adds an extra touch of hearty flavor...that's one reason it's one of my husband's favorites.

1 pound ground beef
1 medium onion, chopped
2 green onions, sliced
1/4 teaspoon dried basil
1/2 teaspoon dry mustard
2 teaspoons chopped fresh garlic
1 can (17 ounces) whole kernel corn, drained
1 can (11 ounces) condensed tomato bisque soup, undiluted
3/4 teaspoon salt
1/2 teaspoon pepper
1/4 cup grated Parmesan cheese
2-1/2 cups hot mashed potatoes
6 slices process cheese

In a skillet, brown ground beef; drain. Add the onion; saute until transparent. Stir in basil, mustard, garlic, corn and tomato soup; simmer for 10-15 minutes. Add salt, pepper and cheese. Spoon into a 13-in. x 9-in. x 2-in. baking dish. Top with mashed potatoes; cover with cheese slices. Bake at 275°, uncovered, for 40 minutes. **Yield:** 4 servings.

CHUCK WAGON MAC

Novella Cook, Hinton, West Virginia

If you like, you can vary this dish by using a macaroni and cheese mix with wheel- or shell-shaped pasta instead of the usual "elbows". Or try white cheddar or Mexican-style macaroni and cheese mixes.

1 package (7-1/4 ounces) macaroni and cheese dinner mix
1 pound ground beef
1/2 cup sliced celery
1/4 cup chopped green pepper
1/4 cup chopped onion
1 can (15 to 16 ounces) whole kernel corn, drained
1 can (15 ounces) tomato sauce
1/2 teaspoon salt
1/4 teaspoon pepper
Chopped fresh parsley

Prepare macaroni and cheese according to package directions; set aside. In a skillet, brown ground beef with celery, green pepper and onion until the beef is browned and the vegetables are tender; drain. Stir in corn, tomato sauce, salt and pepper. Stir in macaroni and cheese. Pour into a greased 12-in. x 8-in. x 2-in. baking dish. Bake at 350° for 15-20 minutes or until heated through. Garnish with parsley. **Yield:** 6-8 servings.

OVEN PORCUPINES

Shelly Ryun, Malvern, Iowa

I've always remembered these from my school days...so I searched until I found the recipe that was just like I remembered. This is it!

1 pound lean ground beef
1/2 cup uncooked long grain rice
1/2 cup water
1/3 cup chopped onion
1 teaspoon salt
1/4 teaspoon garlic powder
1/2 teaspoon pepper
1 can (15 ounces) tomato sauce
1 cup water
2 teaspoons Worcestershire sauce

Combine first 7 ingredients; shape into 12 balls. Place meat balls in an ungreased 8-in square baking dish. Combine remaining ingredients; pour over meatballs. Cover with foil and bake at 350° for 1 hour. Uncover; bake 15 minutes longer. **Yield:** 4 servings.

BEEF PASTITSIO

Sharon Drys, Shelburne, Ontario
(PICTURED AT LEFT)

My children love this dish, and it reheats beautifully...when we do have any left over, that is!

>   1 pound ground beef
>   1 cup chopped onion
>   1 can (15 ounces) tomato sauce
> 1/2 teaspoon salt
> 1/2 teaspoon dried oregano
> 1/4 teaspoon pepper
>   1 garlic clove, minced
>   2 cups uncooked elbow macaroni
>   1 cup (4 ounces) shredded cheddar cheese
>   1 egg, beaten

CHEESE SAUCE:
>   3 tablespoons butter *or* margarine, melted
>   3 tablespoons all-purpose flour
> 1-1/2 cups milk
> 1/2 teaspoon salt
>   1 cup (4 ounces) shredded cheddar cheese

In a skillet, cook beef and onion until meat is browned and onion is tender; drain. Stir in tomato sauce, salt, oregano, pepper and garlic. Cover and simmer for 15 minutes. Meanwhile, cook macaroni according to package directions; drain and rinse. Combine macaroni, cheese and egg; set aside. For cheese sauce, melt butter in a heavy saucepan. Stir in flour; cook until smooth and bubbly. Stir in milk; cook and stir for 5 minutes or until smooth and thickened. Remove from the heat and stir in salt and cheese. Spoon half of the macaroni mixture into the bottom of a greased 13-in. x 9-in. x 2-in. baking dish. Cover with meat mixture; top with remaining macaroni. Spread sauce over the top. Bake at 350°, uncovered, for 30 minutes or until heated through. Let stand 5-10 minutes before serving. **Yield:** 6-8 servings.

ZUCCHINI ITALIANO

Sandy Robideau, Eureka, Montana
(PICTURED AT LEFT)

When zucchini is plentiful in my garden, I slice and parboil it, then freeze it in 4-cup containers for recipes like this. It saves time—and lets us enjoy fresh zucchini year-round!

>   4 cups thinly sliced zucchini
> Water
>   1 pound ground beef
>   1 garlic clove, minced
> 1/2 cup chopped onion
>   1 cup cooked rice
>   1 can (8 ounces) tomato sauce
> 1/2 teaspoon dried oregano
> 1/2 teaspoon salt
> 1/4 teaspoon pepper
>   1 egg, beaten

> 1/2 cup cottage cheese
> 1/2 cup shredded cheddar cheese

Cook zucchini in boiling water for 2-3 minutes or until almost tender. Drain well; set aside. In a skillet, brown beef, garlic and onion; drain off fat. Stir in rice, tomato sauce, oregano, salt and pepper. Simmer for 10 minutes. In a small bowl, combine egg and cottage cheese. Layer half of the zucchini slices in a greased 8-in. square baking dish, overlapping slices as needed. Spoon meat mixture over zucchini; dollop cottage cheese mixture over meat. Top with remaining zucchini slices. Bake, uncovered, at 350° for 25 minutes or until heated through. Sprinkle cheddar cheese around edges; bake an additional 2-3 minutes or until the cheese melts. **Yield:** 4 servings.

MARZETTI

Margaret Adams, North Vernon, Indiana
(PICTURED AT LEFT)

I got this recipe from a friend, who got it from her aunt, who got it from...who knows? Whatever the original source, it's a tasty favorite that's a cinch to make.

>   1 pound ground beef
>   1 large onion, chopped
> 1/2 green pepper, chopped
>   1 can (10-3/4 ounces) condensed cream of mushroom soup, undiluted
>   1 can (10-3/4 ounces) condensed tomato soup, undiluted
>   1 can (6 ounces) tomato paste
>   1 teaspoon salt
> 1/4 teaspoon dried oregano
> 1/4 teaspoon pepper
> 1/3 cup water
>   1 tablespoon Worcestershire sauce
>   8 ounces wide noodles, cooked and drained
>   1 cup (4 ounces) shredded cheddar cheese

Brown ground beef, onion and green pepper; drain off fat. Stir in the next nine ingredients. Spoon into a greased 3-qt. casserole; top with cheese. Cover and bake at 350° for 45 minutes. **Yield:** 4-6 servings.

BEEF AND WILD RICE CASSEROLE

Pamela Petite, Gardnerville, Nevada

This recipe, one of my husband's childhood favorites, was given to me by his grandmother.

> 1-1/2 pounds ground beef
>   1 medium onion, chopped
>   1 cup uncooked wild rice, rinsed
>   1 can (10-3/4 ounces) condensed cream of mushroom soup, undiluted
>   1 can (10-3/4 ounces) condensed chicken noodle soup, undiluted
>   2 soup cans water

In a skillet, brown ground beef with onion until the beef is browned and the onion is tender; drain. Place in a 3-qt. casserole. Add all remaining ingredients and mix well. Cover and bake at 375° for 1 hour and 20 minutes, stirring often. **Yield:** 6-8 servings.

FAMILY PLEASERS. Pictured at left, clockwise from bottom: Zucchini Italiano, Beef Pastitsio, Marzetti (all recipes on this page).

■ ■ ■

RED AND GREEN CASSEROLE
Joan Latourette, Harrisburg, Pennsylvania

This recipe is at least 100 years old. Make it once, and you'll see why it has been a favorite for over a century!

1-1/2 pounds ground beef
   2 medium onions, chopped
   1 green pepper, chopped
   1 sweet red pepper, chopped
   2 cans (10-3/4 ounces *each*) condensed
      tomato soup, undiluted
 1/4 cup water
   1 teaspoon sugar
 1/2 teaspoon chili powder
Salt and pepper to taste
   8 ounces wide noodles, cooked and drained
   1 cup (4 ounces) shredded cheddar cheese

In a skillet, cook beef, onions and peppers until vegetables are tender. Drain well. Stir in soup, water, sugar, chili powder, salt and pepper. Stir in noodles. Turn into a greased 13-in. x 9-in. x 2-in. baking dish. Sprinkle with cheese. Bake, uncovered, at 350° for 30 minutes. **Yield:** 4-6 servings.

■ ■ ■

BAKED ZITI WITH FRESH TOMATOES
Barbara Johnson, Decker, Indiana

I prepare the sauce ahead of time, so it saves precious moments when we come in after working out in the fields!

   1 pound ground beef
   1 cup chopped onion
   8 cups blanched, peeled and chopped fresh
      tomatoes (about 3 pounds)
   1 teaspoon dried basil
1-1/2 teaspoons salt
 1/4 teaspoon pepper
   8 ounces ziti *or* any medium tubular pasta,
      cooked and drained
   2 cups (8 ounces) shredded mozzarella
      cheese, *divided*
   2 tablespoons grated Parmesan cheese

In a skillet, brown beef and onion; drain. Stir in tomatoes, basil, salt and pepper. Simmer for 45 minutes, stirring occasionally. Stir in ziti and 1 cup mozzarella. Spoon into a greased 2-1/2-qt. casserole; sprinkle with Parmesan and remaining mozzarella. Cover and bake at 350° for 15 minutes. Uncover; bake 15 minutes longer or until heated through. **Yield:** 6 servings.

■ ■ ■

MANICOTTI
Judy Wulf, Hancock, Minnesota

A friend served this for supper when I visited, and she placed individual servings on a bed of lettuce, then sprinkled them with cheese...it was both pretty and delicious.

   1 pound ground beef
 1/4 cup chopped onion
 1/4 cup chopped green pepper

   1 teaspoon salt
 1/4 teaspoon pepper
   1 tablespoon chopped fresh parsley
   1 can (4 ounces) mushroom stems and pieces,
      drained
   1 egg, beaten
 1/4 cup milk
 1/2 cup seasoned dry bread crumbs
   8 ounces (14 tubes) manicotti, cooked
      and drained
   1 jar (32 ounces) spaghetti sauce, *divided*
   1 cup (4 ounces) shredded process cheese

In a skillet, cook ground beef, onion, green pepper, salt and pepper until vegetables are tender; drain. Stir in parsley, mushrooms, egg, milk and bread crumbs; mix well. Stuff filling into manicotti shells. Pour half of spaghetti sauce into a greased 13-in. x 9-in. x 2-in. baking dish. Place shells on sauce; top with remaining sauce. Cover and bake at 350° for 25-30 minutes. Uncover and sprinkle with cheese. Return to oven for 5 minutes or until cheese is melted. **Yield:** 6-8 servings.

■ ■ ■

CHEESY CASSEROLE
Mary Elizabeth Golding, Colorado Springs, Colorado

The comforting flavors of old-time country foods make this a favorite with my family.

   1 pound ground beef
   1 can (10-3/4 ounces) condensed tomato
      soup, undiluted
   1 teaspoon salt
 1/8 teaspoon pepper
   1 cup small curd cottage cheese
   1 cup (8 ounces) sour cream
   6 to 8 green onions with tops, sliced
   8 ounces medium noodles, cooked and drained
   1 cup (4 ounces) shredded cheddar cheese

In a skillet, brown beef; drain. Add soup, salt and pepper; simmer for 5 minutes. Remove from the heat. In a large mixing bowl, combine cottage cheese, sour cream, green onions and noodles. Layer noodle mixture alternately with meat sauce in a greased 2-qt. casserole. Cover and bake at 350° for 25 minutes. Sprinkle with cheese; return to oven for 5-10 minutes or until cheese melts. **Yield:** 6-8 servings.

■ ■ ■

PIZZA CASSEROLE
Judy Chandler, Franklin, Kentucky

I discovered this recipe in the reader's exhange page of our local electric cooperative's magazine. Serve it whenever you've got a crowd to please!

   1 pound ground beef
   1 package (3-1/2 ounces) sliced pepperoni
   1 onion, chopped
   1 green pepper, chopped
   1 can (4 ounces) sliced mushrooms, drained
   7 ounces vermicelli, cooked and drained
 1/3 cup butter *or* margarine, melted
   1 can (16 ounces) tomato sauce, *divided*

1 cup (4 ounces) shredded Swiss cheese
4 cups (16 ounces) shredded mozzarella
    cheese
1/2 teaspoon dried oregano
1/2 teaspoon dried basil
Green pepper rings, optional

In a skillet, cook ground beef, pepperoni, onion and green pepper until beef is browned and vegetables are tender. Drain. Stir in mushrooms; set aside. Combine vermicelli and butter in a 13-in. x 9-in. x 2-in. baking dish; toss noodles to coat evenly. Pour 1 cup of tomato sauce over noodles. Spoon half of the meat mixture over noodles. Combine Swiss and mozzarella cheeses; sprinkle half over meat mixture. Sprinkle with oregano and basil. Repeat with remaining meat and cheese mixtures. Pour remaining tomato sauce over cheese layer. Bake, uncovered, at 350° for 25-30 minutes or until bubbly. Garnish with green pepper rings if desired. **Yield:** 8-10 servings.

■ ■ ■

MEAT-AND-POTATO SQUARES
Wanda Kaney, Williston, South Carolina

My children enjoy topping these with ketchup—they say it's like having hamburgers and fries without the buns!

1 pound ground beef
1 egg
1/4 cup milk
1 teaspoon salt
1 teaspoon prepared mustard
1/4 teaspoon pepper
1 cup dry bread crumbs
1/2 cup chopped onion
1 package (16 ounces) frozen shoestring
    french fries
Ketchup, optional

Combine first eight ingredients in a large mixing bowl; mix well. Set aside. Place half of the potatoes in the bottom of a greased 8-in. square baking dish. Spread meat mixture evenly over potatoes. Firmly pat the remaining potatoes on top. Bake, uncovered, at 400° for 30 minutes or until the meat is cooked and the potatoes are lightly browned. Cut into squares. Serve with ketchup if desired. **Yield:** 6 servings.

■ ■ ■

SWEDISH MEATBALLS
Kathy Ringel, Saline, Michigan

The allspice and nutmeg—plus a hint of dill—are what give these tender meatballs their special old-world flavor.

2 eggs, beaten
1/2 cup milk
1 cup dry bread crumbs
2 teaspoons salt
1/2 teaspoon pepper
1-1/2 teaspoons dried dill weed
1/4 teaspoon ground allspice
1/4 teaspoon ground nutmeg
1 cup chopped onion
2 tablespoons butter *or* margarine

2 pounds ground beef
1/2 pound ground pork
SAUCE:
1/4 cup butter *or* margarine
1/2 cup all-purpose flour
2 cans (14-1/2 ounces *each*) beef broth
1 pint heavy cream
1/2 teaspoon dried dill weed
1/2 teaspoon salt
1/4 teaspoon pepper
Fresh dill sprigs, optional

In a large mixing bowl, combine eggs, milk, bread crumbs and seasonings; set aside. In a skillet, saute onion in butter until soft; add to egg mixture. Add beef and ground pork; mix well. Cover and refrigerate for 1 hour. Shape meat mixture into 1-1/4- to 1-1/2-in. balls. Place on a jelly roll pan. Bake, uncovered, at 350° for 20-25 minutes. Remove from oven and place in a 3-qt. casserole. For sauce, melt butter in a saucepan; stir in flour to form a smooth paste. Gradually stir in broth; bring to a boil, stirring constantly. Reduce heat; stir in cream, dill, salt and pepper. If a thicker sauce is desired, continue cooking 10-15 minutes longer, stirring occasionally. Pour sauce over meatballs. Bake, uncovered, at 350° for 40-45 minutes or until heated through and bubbly. Garnish with fresh dill if desired. **Yield:** 10-12 servings.

■ ■ ■

ZUCCHINI PIZZA CASSEROLE
Emma Gayle Hageman, Waucoma, Iowa

The taste of pizza in this dish—and the goodness of garden produce—makes it a surefire hit with folks of all ages!

4 cups shredded unpeeled zucchini (about
    3 medium)
1/2 teaspoon salt
1 cup (4 ounces) shredded mozzarella
    cheese, *divided*
1 cup (4 ounces) shredded cheddar cheese,
    divided
1/2 cup grated Parmesan cheese
2 eggs
1 pound ground beef
1/2 cup chopped onion
1 can (8 ounces) tomato sauce
1/4 teaspoon garlic powder
1/4 teaspoon dried oregano
1 cup chopped green pepper
2 cans (4 ounces *each*) mushrooms, drained

Place zucchini in a double thickness of cheesecloth; sprinkle with salt. Let stand for 10 minutes. Gather ends of cheesecloth and squeeze out as much liquid as possible. In a bowl, combine zucchini, 1/2 cup mozzarella cheese, 1/2 cup cheddar cheese, Parmesan cheese and eggs. Press into the bottom of a greased 13-in. x 9-in. x 2-in. baking dish. Bake, uncovered, at 400° for 20 minutes or until crust is set. Meanwhile, in a large skillet, brown ground beef and onion; drain. Stir in tomato sauce, garlic powder, and oregano; bring to a boil. Spoon over crust. Top with green pepper and mushrooms; sprinkle with remaining cheeses. Bake 25-35 minutes more or until heated through and cheeses are melted. **Yield:** 6 servings.

THINK ITALIAN! Clockwise from top right: Italian Stuffed Shells (p. 54), Stuffed Zucchini (p. 55), Baked Mostaccioli (p. 55), White Lasagna (p. 54), and Pancake Lasagna (p. 54).

ITALIAN STUFFED SHELLS

Beverly Austin, Fulton, Missouri
(PICTURED ON PAGE 52)

A dear friend first brought over this casserole when I was recovering from an accident. Now I take it to other friends' homes and to potlucks, because it's always a big hit!

1 pound ground beef
1 cup chopped onion
1 garlic clove, minced
2 cups hot water
1 can (12 ounces) tomato paste
1 tablespoon beef bouillon granules
1-1/2 teaspoons dried oregano
1 carton (16 ounces) cottage cheese
2 cups (8 ounces) shredded mozzarella
  cheese, *divided*
1/2 cup grated Parmesan cheese
1 egg, beaten
24 jumbo shell noodles, cooked and drained

In a large skillet, brown beef, onion and garlic; drain well. Stir in water, tomato paste, bouillon and oregano; simmer, uncovered, about 30 minutes. Meanwhile, in a medium bowl, combine cottage cheese, 1 cup mozzarella, Parmesan cheese and egg; mix well. Stuff shells with cheese mixture; arrange in a 13-in. x 9-in. x 2-in. baking dish. Pour meat sauce over shells. Cover and bake at 350° for 30 minutes. Uncover, sprinkle with remaining mozzarella cheese. Bake 5 minutes longer or until the cheese is melted. **Yield:** 6-8 servings.

PANCAKE LASAGNA

Nancy Reed, Battle Creek, Michigan
(PICTURED ON PAGE 53)

Take this dish along to your next potluck supper, and don't be surprised when there isn't a morsel left over—it's that good! It's also a unique way to serve lasagna.

1 pound ground beef
1 cup cottage cheese
1 can (6 ounces) tomato paste
1 tomato paste can water
2 tablespoons dried minced onion
1 teaspoon dried basil
3/4 teaspoon garlic salt
1/2 teaspoon dried oregano
1/4 teaspoon pepper
2 eggs
2/3 cup milk
1/2 cup all-purpose flour
1/4 teaspoon salt
2 cups (8 ounces) shredded mozzarella
  cheese
1/2 cup grated Parmesan cheese

In a skillet, brown ground beef; drain. Process cottage cheese in a blender or food processor until smooth. Stir into ground beef with seasonings; set aside. In a mixing bowl, beat eggs, milk, flour and salt. Pour 1/3 cup batter into a greased 9-in. skillet, tilting to cover the bottom of the pan. When set and lightly browned, flip the pancake to brown the other side. Remove from pan and place on paper towel; repeat with remaining batter. Place one pancake in a 10-in. pie plate. Spread with one-fourth of the meat mixture, 1/2 cup mozzarella cheese and 1 tablespoon Parmesan cheese. Repeat layers with remaining pancakes and ingredients, ending with the cheeses. Bake, uncovered, at 375° for 25-30 minutes. **Yield:** 4-6 servings.

WHITE LASAGNA

James Hospodka, Omaha, Nebraska
(PICTURED ON PAGE 53)

I love to cook—and I love this recipe! Its one-of-a-kind taste is a delicious change of pace from "regular" lasagna.

1 pound ground beef
1 cup finely chopped celery
1 cup finely chopped onion
1 garlic clove, minced
2 teaspoons dried basil
1 teaspoon dried oregano
1/2 teaspoon dried Italian seasoning
1/2 teaspoon salt
1/2 teaspoon pepper
1 cup light cream
1 package (3 ounces) cream cheese, cubed
2 cups (8 ounces) shredded cheddar cheese
1 package (7 ounces) Gouda cheese,
  shredded
1 carton (16 ounces) cottage cheese
1 egg, beaten
12 ounces sliced *or* shredded mozzarella
  cheese
8 ounces lasagna noodles, cooked and
  drained
Chopped fresh parsley

In a skillet, cook ground beef with celery, onion and garlic until meat is browned and vegetables are tender; drain. Stir in basil, oregano, Italian seasoning, salt and pepper. Stir in cream and cream cheese; cook and stir over low heat until cheese is melted. Gradually add cheddar and Gouda cheese, stirring until cheese is melted; remove from the heat. Combine cottage cheese and egg; set aside. Layer half of lasagna noodles in a greased 13-in. x 9-in. x 2-in. baking dish. Top with half of the meat sauce, half of the cottage cheese mixture and half of the mozzarella cheese. Repeat layers with remaining ingredients. Bake at 375°, uncovered, for 30-35 minutes. Sprinkle with parsley. Let stand 10 minutes before serving. **Yield:** 14-16 servings.

■ ■ ■
STUFFED ZUCCHINI
Linda Logan, Warren, Ohio
(PICTURED ON PAGE 52)

As a home gardener, I'm always looking for tasty ways to use my huge crop of zucchini. This is one of my favorites!

    4 to 5 medium zucchini
1-1/2 pounds lean ground beef
1-1/2 cups soft bread crumbs
    1 tablespoon minced fresh parsley
 1/4 cup grated Parmesan cheese
    1 small onion, chopped
    1 egg, beaten
    1 teaspoon salt
 1/2 teaspoon pepper
    1 can (10-3/4 ounces) condensed tomato
       soup, undiluted
 1/2 cup water

Wash and trim the ends of zucchini. Cut in half lengthwise; scoop out pulp. Finely chop pulp. In a mixing bowl, combine pulp, ground beef, bread crumbs, parsley, Parmesan cheese, onion and egg. Add seasonings. Fill zucchini shells with meat mixture. Place in a 13-in. x 9-in. x 2-in. baking dish. Combine tomato soup and water; pour over zucchini. Bake at 350° for 45-50 minutes. **Yield:** 8-10 servings.

■ ■ ■
BAKED MOSTACCIOLI
Darlene Carlson, Jamestown, North Dakota
(PICTURED ON PAGE 53)

I came across this recipe several years ago, and it has been a hit with my family ever since. My children especially enjoy the unique noodles! It's ideal to take to our church potlucks, because it serves a large group.

    8 ounces mostaccioli noodles
1-1/2 pounds ground beef
 1/2 cup chopped onion
    1 garlic clove, minced
    1 can (28 ounces) tomatoes with juice, cut up
    1 can (8 ounces) tomato sauce
    1 can (6 ounces) tomato paste
    1 can (4 ounces) sliced mushrooms, drained
 1/2 cup water
    1 to 1-1/4 teaspoons salt
    1 teaspoon sugar
    1 teaspoon dried basil
 1/8 teaspoon pepper
    1 bay leaf
    2 cups (8 ounces) shredded mozzarella
       cheese
 1/2 cup grated Parmesan cheese

Cook mostaccioli according to package directions; drain and set aside. In a large saucepan, brown ground beef, onion and garlic; drain. Stir in tomatoes, tomato sauce and paste, mushrooms, water, salt, sugar, basil, pepper and bay leaf. Bring to a boil; reduce heat and simmer for 30 minutes, stirring occasionally. Remove bay leaf. Stir in mostaccioli. Spoon half into a 13-in. x 9-in. x 2-in. baking dish. Sprinkle with mozzarella cheese; layer with remaining meat mixture. Sprinkle with Parmesan

cheese. Cover with foil. Bake at 350° for 30-35 minutes or until heated through. Let stand 5 minutes before serving. **Yield:** 10-12 servings.

■ ■ ■
POTATO LASAGNA
Gwen Johnson, Willmar, Minnesota

Potatoes in place of lasagna noodles? Yes—and this is so hearty, it satisfies even my two teenage sons' appetites!

1-1/2 pounds ground beef
    1 medium onion, chopped
    1 jar (32 ounces) spaghetti sauce
    1 teaspoon dried basil
    1 teaspoon dried oregano
    1 teaspoon sugar
 1/2 teaspoon salt
 1/4 teaspoon pepper
 1/3 cup water
    1 can (4 ounces) mushroom pieces and
       stems, drained
    5 medium potatoes, peeled and thinly sliced
    2 cups (8 ounces) shredded mozzarella
       cheese

In a skillet, brown ground beef with onion; drain. Stir in spaghetti sauce, seasonings, water and mushrooms; mix well. Pour half into a 13-in. x 9-in. x 2-in. baking dish. Cover with potatoes. Pour remaining sauce over potatoes. Cover tightly with foil. Bake at 350° for 1 hour and 15 minutes or until potatoes are tender. Sprinkle with mozzarella cheese; return to oven for another 10 minutes or until the cheese is melted. **Yield:** 10-12 servings.

■ ■ ■
BEEF CRESCENT LOAF
Mabel Billington, Mayville, Wisconsin

Try this family-pleasing recipe and serve it with a salad and raw vegetable sticks.

1-1/2 pounds ground beef
 1/2 cup chopped onion
 3/4 cup chopped green pepper
    2 cans (11 ounces *each*) condensed cheddar
       cheese soup, undiluted
    1 tablespoon Worcestershire sauce
 1/2 teaspoon salt
 1/4 teaspoon pepper
    1 can (8 ounces) refrigerated crescent rolls
 1/2 cup shredded cheddar cheese

In a skillet, brown ground beef with onion; drain. Stir in green pepper, soup, Worcestershire sauce, salt and pepper; set aside. On an ungreased baking sheet, separate crescent dough into 2 large rectangles. Join the longer sides together. Press edges and perforations together to form a 12-in. x 7-in. rectangle. Spread half of the meat mixture down the center of the rectangle to within 1-in. of edges. Set aside meat mixture . Fold longer sides of dough over meat mixture to center; seal ends. Bake at 375° for 15 minutes. Remove from oven and spoon remaining meat mixture down center of loaf. Sprinkle with cheddar cheese; bake 10 minutes longer or until loaf is golden brown and cheese is melted. **Yield:** 6 servings.

BARBECUED BEEF AND BEANS

Mary Lou Ringhand, Albany, Wisconsin
(PICTURED AT LEFT)

I like to make this dish for church potlucks. It's great for large groups. I always include at least six kinds of beans, but they're not the same every time.

- 1 pound ground beef
- 1 medium onion, finely diced
- 1 garlic clove, minced
- 1/2 cup barbecue sauce
- 1/2 cup ketchup
- 1/4 cup molasses
- 1/2 cup packed brown sugar
- 1 jar (32 ounces) northern navy beans
- 1 can (15 ounces) garbanzo beans
- 1 can (16 ounces) cut green beans, drained
- 1 can (16 ounces) red kidney beans
- 1 can (17 ounces) lima beans
- 1 can (28 ounces) baked beans

In a skillet, brown beef with onion and garlic until beef is no longer pink. Drain; place in a large greased roaster or casserole. Stir in barbecue sauce, ketchup, molasses and brown sugar. Add all beans and mix well. Bake, uncovered, at 325° for 30 minutes. Cover and bake another 30 minutes. **Yield:** 8-10 servings.

SHEPHERD'S PIE

Valerie Merrill, Topeka, Kansas
(PICTURED AT LEFT)

This economical dish comes from a friend who was a whiz at pinching pennies without sacrificing hearty flavor.

- 2-1/2 pounds potatoes, peeled and cooked
- 1 to 1-1/2 cups (8 to 12 ounces) sour cream
- Salt and pepper to taste
- 2 pounds ground beef
- 1/2 cup chopped onion
- 1 medium sweet red pepper, chopped
- 1 teaspoon garlic salt
- 1 can (10-3/4 ounces) condensed cream of mushroom soup, undiluted
- 1 can (16 ounces) whole kernel corn, drained
- 1/2 cup milk
- 2 tablespoons butter *or* margarine, melted
- Chopped fresh parsley, optional

Mash potatoes with sour cream. Add salt and pepper; set aside. In a skillet, cook beef with onion and red pepper until meat is brown and vegetables are tender; drain. Stir garlic salt into meat mixture. Add soup, corn and milk; mix well. Spread meat mixture in a 13-in. x 9-in. x 2-in. baking dish. Top with mashed potatoes; drizzle with butter. Bake, uncovered, at 350° for

SATISFACTION GUARANTEED! Pictured at left, clockwise from top: Barbecued Beef and Beans, Shepherd's Pie and Cheesy Stuffed Peppers (all recipes on this page).

30-35 minutes or until heated through. For additional browning, place under broiler for a few minutes. Sprinkle with parsley if desired. **Yield:** 8-10 servings.

CHEESY STUFFED PEPPERS

Betty DeRaad, Sioux Falls, South Dakota
(PICTURED AT LEFT)

This is my favorite summertime supper because I can use peppers and tomatoes fresh from my garden.

- 6 medium green peppers
- 1-1/2 pounds ground beef
- 1 medium onion, chopped
- 1/2 teaspoon salt
- 2 cups (8 ounces) shredded cheddar cheese
- 2-1/2 cups chopped tomatoes (3 medium)
- 1-1/2 cups cooked rice

Cut tops from peppers and remove seeds. Place in a saucepan and cover with water; bring to a boil and boil for 6-8 minutes. Meanwhile, brown beef, onion and salt in a skillet. Drain fat. Cool slightly; add cheese, tomatoes and rice. Drain peppers and stuff with meat mixture. Place in a baking dish. Bake, uncovered, at 350° for 20 minutes. **Yield:** 6 servings.

CABBAGE ROLLS

Mary Lea Schmidt, Anahim Lake, British Columbia

This delicious recipe was given to me by a special friend— she included it in a collection of her family's favorites that she gave us as a unique wedding present.

- 1 medium head cabbage
- 1-1/2 pounds lean ground beef
- 1/2 cup uncooked instant rice
- 1/2 cup finely minced onion
- 1 egg, lightly beaten
- 1 teaspoon salt
- 1/2 teaspoon garlic powder
- 1/2 teaspoon pepper
- SAUCE:
- 1 can (8 ounces) tomato sauce
- 1/3 cup ketchup
- 2 tablespoons brown sugar
- 2 tablespoons vinegar
- 1/4 teaspoon salt
- 1/4 teaspoon pepper

Remove core from the cabbage. Place cabbage in a large saucepan and cover with water. Bring to a boil; after about 3 minutes, outer leaves should be softened enough to remove. Return to a boil; reduce heat and simmer until leaves are tender, about 10-15 minutes. Remove the tough center stalk from each leaf; reserve extra leaves and line a large baking dish with them. (If leaves for rolling are too brittle, return to boiling water for 1-2 minutes.) Combine meat, rice, onion, egg and seasonings; mix well. Place about 2 tablespoons of meat mixture on each cabbage leaf. Roll toward the stalk, tucking in sides. Place rolls, seam side down, in baking dish. Combine all sauce ingredients; pour over rolls. Cover and bake at 350° for 1-1/2 to 1-3/4 hours. **Yield:** 6-8 servings.

Meat Pies & Pizza

ZESTY POTATO PIZZA
Marilyn Stroud, Larsen, Wisconsin
(PICTURED AT LEFT)

I originally invented this recipe for the state agriculture department's "Potato Recipe Contest"—and won first place!

CRUST:
- 6 medium potatoes, peeled, cooked and mashed
- 1/3 cup sour cream
- 1/3 cup shredded mozzarella cheese
- 1 egg, beaten
- Salt and pepper to taste
- 2 teaspoons dry bread crumbs

TOPPING:
- 1 pound ground beef
- 1 can (12 ounces) luncheon meat, cubed
- 1 small onion, chopped
- 1 can (8 ounces) pizza sauce
- 1 cup (4 ounces) shredded mozzarella cheese
- 2 tablespoons grated Parmesan cheese

For crust, beat together hot mashed potatoes, sour cream, mozzarella cheese and egg in a mixing bowl. Season to taste with salt and pepper. Spread potato mixture onto a 12-in. pizza pan, building up the edges to form sides of a pizza crust. Sprinkle with bread crumbs. Bake at 350° for 20 minutes. Meanwhile, for topping, brown beef, luncheon meat and onion in a skillet; drain well. Stir in pizza sauce; set aside. Remove crust from oven; increase temperature to 400°. Spoon topping mixture evenly over crust. Sprinkle with mozzarella and Parmesan cheeses. Bake another 10 minutes. Cut into wedges and serve with forks. **Yield:** 4-6 servings.

PRIAZZO
Carol Gillespie, Chambersburg, Pennsylvania
(PICTURED AT LEFT)

This stuffed pizza is a real treat—and the frozen bread dough makes it a snap to prepare as well.

- 1/2 pound ground beef
- 1 small onion, chopped
- 1 small green pepper, chopped
- 2 loaves (1 pound *each*) frozen bread dough, thawed
- 4 cups (16 ounces) shredded mozzarella cheese, *divided*
- 18 slices pepperoni
- 1 can (4 ounces) sliced mushrooms, drained
- 1 can (14 ounces) pizza sauce

In a skillet, brown ground beef, onion and green pepper; drain. Divide one loaf of bread dough in half. Press over the bottom and up the sides of two 9-in. greased pie plates. Sprinkle each pie with 1-1/2 cups of mozzarella cheese. Divide beef mixture and spoon over cheese. Top with pepperoni and mushrooms. Divide remaining loaf of bread; form into two 10-in. circles. Cover each pie with dough; crimp edges to seal. Spread half of the pizza sauce onto each pie. Sprinkle with remaining cheese. Bake at 400° for 25-30 minutes. **Yield:** 12-16 servings.

OLD-WORLD PIZZA
Linda Hovey, Mondovi, Wisconsin
(PICTURED AT LEFT)

For our family, there's no pizza as satisfying as this one with its yeast-raised crust and old-fashioned flavor.

- 1 package (1/4 ounce) active dry yeast
- 1 cup warm water (105° to 115°)
- 1 teaspoon sugar
- 1 teaspoon salt
- 2 tablespoons vegetable oil
- 2-1/2 cups all-purpose flour
- 1 can (8 ounces) pizza sauce
- 1 pound ground beef, browned and drained
- 1-1/2 cups (6 ounces) shredded mozzarella cheese
- 1-1/2 cups (6 ounces) shredded cheddar cheese
- 2 cups sliced pepperoni
- 1/3 cup grated Parmesan cheese

In a mixing bowl, dissolve yeast in water. Stir in sugar, salt, oil and flour. Beat vigorously 20 strokes. Cover and let rest about 15 minutes. With buttered fingers, pat crust into a greased 15-in. x 10-in. x 1-in. baking pan. Cover with pizza sauce. Top with next four ingredients. Sprinkle with Parmesan cheese. Bake at 425° for 15-20 minutes or until crust and cheese are lightly browned. **Yield:** 8-12 servings.

TACO CRESCENTS
Eleanor Lapen, Chicago, Illinois

These are easy to make—and freeze well, too. Kids love 'em!

- 3/4 pound ground beef
- 1/4 cup chopped onion
- 1 package (1-1/4 ounces) taco seasoning
- 1 can (4-1/4 ounces) chopped ripe olives, drained
- 2 eggs, lightly beaten
- 1/2 cup shredded cheddar cheese
- 2 tubes (8 ounces *each*) refrigerated crescent rolls

In a skillet, brown beef with onion; drain. Add taco seasoning and olives; mix well and set aside to cool. Add eggs and cheese; mix well. On a baking sheet, separate dough. Place 2 tablespoons of meat mixture onto each triangle. Roll and shape into crescents. Bake at 375° for 10-15 minutes or until lightly browned. **Yield:** 8 servings.

PIZZA PARTY. Pictured at left, top to bottom: Zesty Potato Pizza, Priazzo, Old-World Pizza (recipes above).

BIEROCKS

Ellen Batt, Hoisington, Kansas
(PICTURED AT RIGHT)

This is an old German recipe handed down from generation to generation, using foods grown or raised on the family farm. I remember helping my grandmother make these when I could barely see over the kitchen table!

DOUGH:
- 10 to 11 cups all-purpose flour, *divided*
- 1 package (1/4 ounce) active dry yeast
- 1/2 cup sugar
- 2 teaspoons salt
- 2-1/2 cups water
- 1 cup milk
- 1/2 cup butter *or* margarine
- 2 eggs

FILLING:
- 2 pounds ground beef
- 1 large onion, chopped
- 2 teaspoons salt
- 1 teaspoon ground white pepper
- 2 pounds shredded cabbage, cooked and drained

For dough, in a large mixing bowl, combine 4 cups of flour, yeast, sugar and salt; mix well and set aside. In a saucepan, heat water, milk and butter just until butter melts. Remove from heat and cool to 120°-130°. Combine with flour mixture; add eggs. Using an electric mixer, blend at low speed until moistened then beat at medium speed for 3 minutes. By hand, gradually stir in enough remaining flour to make a firm dough. Knead on a floured surface about 10 minutes. Place in a greased bowl, turning once to grease top. Cover and let rise in a warm place until doubled, about 1 hour. Punch dough down; let rise again until almost doubled. Meanwhile, for the filling, brown beef with onion, salt and pepper; drain. Mix together with cabbage; set aside. Divide the dough into fourths. Roll each piece into a 15-in. x 10-in. rectangle. Cut into 5-in. squares. Spoon 1/3 to 1/2 cup of filling onto each square. Bring the four corners up over the filling; pinch together to seal. Repeat with remaining dough and filling. Place on greased baking sheets. Bake at 375° for 30 minutes or until brown. **Yield:** 24 servings.

SPAGHETTI PIE

Mary Miller, Hopewell, Pennsylvania
(PICTURED AT RIGHT)

This recipe came to me through a recipe exchange with a friend. It's our favorite way to do something different with pasta without a lot of fuss or exotic ingredients.

CRUST:
- 7 ounces uncooked spaghetti
- 2 tablespoons butter *or* margarine
- 1/3 cup grated Parmesan cheese
- 2 eggs, beaten

FILLING:
- 1 cup cottage cheese
- 1 pound ground beef

- 1/2 cup chopped onion
- 1/4 cup chopped green pepper
- 1 can (16 ounces) diced tomatoes with liquid
- 1 can (6 ounces) tomato paste
- 1 teaspoon sugar
- 1 teaspoon dried oregano
- 1/2 teaspoon garlic salt
- 1/2 cup shredded mozzarella cheese

Cook spaghetti according to package directions; drain. Combine hot spaghetti, butter, Parmesan cheese and eggs in a large bowl. Turn into a greased 10-in. pie plate. Using your fingers, form a crust. Spoon cottage cheese evenly over crust; set aside. In a skillet, cook ground beef, onion and green pepper until beef is browned and onion is tender; drain. Stir in tomatoes, tomato paste, sugar, oregano and garlic salt. Heat through. Pour meat mixture over cottage cheese layer. Bake, uncovered, at 350° for 20 minutes or until set. Sprinkle with mozzarella cheese. Bake 5 minutes longer or until cheese is melted. **Yield:** 6 servings.

BROCCOLI BEEF PIE

Marie Giegerich, Dubuque, Iowa
(PICTURED AT RIGHT)

I received this recipe from my daughter-in-law. It makes a delicious dish for a potluck—everyone loves it!

- 2 cups chopped fresh broccoli
- 1 pound ground beef
- 1 can (4 ounces) sliced mushrooms, drained
- 2 cups (8 ounces) shredded cheddar cheese, *divided*
- 1/3 cup chopped onion
- 2 cups buttermilk biscuit mix
- 1/2 cup water
- 4 eggs
- 1/2 cup milk
- 1/4 cup grated Parmesan cheese
- 1/2 teaspoon salt
- 1/2 teaspoon pepper

In a small saucepan, cook broccoli in a small amount of water until crisp-tender; drain and set aside. In a skillet, brown ground beef, stirring often to crumble; drain. Stir in mushrooms, 1-1/2 cups cheddar cheese and onion. Remove from heat and set aside. Stir together biscuit mix and water to form a soft dough. Add remaining cheddar cheese; stir until blended. With well-floured hands, pat dough into a greased 13-in. x 9-in. x 2-in. baking dish, spreading dough halfway up the sides. Spoon meat mixture over dough and top with broccoli. Combine eggs, milk, Parmesan cheese, salt and pepper; beat well and pour over broccoli. Bake, uncovered, at 350° for 35 minutes or until a knife inserted in the center comes out clean. **Yield:** 8 servings.

SPINACH BEEF PIE: Substitute 2 cups cooked, drained spinach for the broccoli and 2 cups Swiss cheese for the cheddar cheese.

> **BEEF BONANZA.** Pictured at right from top to bottom: Bierocks, Spaghetti Pie and Broccoli Beef Pie (all recipes on this page).

MASHED POTATO PIE

Betty Maschke, Young America, Minnesota

My son enjoys trying new recipes. One weekend, he brought this over, ready to pop into the oven. It's especially good when served with a tossed salad, hot rolls...and brownies or fresh fruit for dessert!

  1 **pound ground beef**
  1 **small onion, chopped**
  1 **can (10-3/4 ounces) condensed cream of chicken soup, undiluted**
  1 **can (10-3/4 ounces) condensed cream of mushroom soup, undiluted**
  1 **can (14-1/2 ounces) green beans, drained**
  1 **can (4 ounces) sliced mushrooms, drained**
6 to 7 **potatoes, peeled, cooked and mashed**
  1 **egg, beaten**
  1 **teaspoon salt**
1/2 **teaspoon pepper**
  1 **can (2.8 ounces) french-fried onions**
1/2 **cup shredded cheddar cheese**

In a skillet, brown ground beef and onion; drain well. Stir in soups, beans and mushrooms. Simmer until heated through. Meanwhile, combine hot mashed potatoes, egg, salt and pepper; mix well. Spread into the bottom and up the sides of a greased 13-in. x 9-in. x 2-in. baking dish or two greased 9-in. pie plates. Spoon ground beef mixture into potato crust. Bake at 350° for 45-50 minutes or until lightly browned. Remove from oven; sprinkle with french-fried onions and cheese. Return to oven for 5 minutes or until cheese is melted. **Yield:** 6-8 servings.

CHEESY HERB PIZZA

Debbie Stieg, Ekalaka, Montana

Before I discovered this recipe, making really good pizza—especially the crust—was difficult. Now I get compliments on this pizza all the time!

  1 **pound ground beef**
  1 **pound bulk pork sausage**
  3 **cups buttermilk biscuit mix**
2/3 **cup water**
  1 **can (8 ounces) tomato sauce**
  1 **can (8-1/4 ounces) tomatoes with liquid, chopped**
  1 **medium onion, diced**
  1 **small green pepper, diced**
1/2 **teaspoon dried thyme**
1/2 **teaspoon dried parsley**
1/2 **teaspoon celery seed**
1/4 **teaspoon minced garlic**
1/2 **teaspoon salt**
1/4 **teaspoon pepper**
1/4 **teaspoon onion salt**
  1 **can (4 ounces) sliced mushrooms, drained**
  2 **cups (8 ounces) shredded cheddar cheese**
2-1/2 **cups (10 ounces) shredded mozzarella cheese**

In a skillet, cook ground beef and sausage; drain well and set aside. In a large mixing bowl, combine biscuit mix

and water. Stir to form a soft dough. Press into a greased 15-in. x 10-in. x 2-in. baking pan. In a saucepan, combine next 11 ingredients. Bring to a boil, reduce heat and simmer 5 minutes; spoon over crust. Crumble meat mixture over sauce; top with mushrooms. Sprinkle with cheddar and mozzarella cheeses. Cover loosely with foil and bake at 350° for 35-40 minutes. Remove foil and bake an additional 5-10 minutes or until the pizza is browned and cheese is melted. **Yield:** 16-18 servings.

POUR PIZZA

Eunice Malin, Montrose, Colorado

I've always liked this recipe—not only for the taste, but for the pourable crust that you don't have to roll out and stretch. The recipe comes from a friend at church.

Cornmeal
  1 **pound ground beef**
  1 **onion, chopped**
  1 **teaspoon salt**
1/4 **teaspoon pepper**
  1 **cup all-purpose flour**
1/4 **teaspoon dried oregano**
  2 **eggs**
2/3 **cup milk**
  1 **can (15 ounces) pizza sauce**
  2 **cups (8 ounces) shredded mozzarella cheese**

Grease a 13-in. x 9-in. x 2-in. baking dish; sprinkle lightly with cornmeal and set aside. In a skillet, lightly brown ground beef and onion; drain. Season with salt and pepper; set aside. In a mixing bowl, combine flour, oregano, eggs and milk. Stir to form a smooth batter and pour into the baking dish. Crumble meat mixture over batter. Bake at 400° for 15-20 minutes. Remove from oven and spoon pizza sauce over meat mixture; sprinkle with cheese. Return to oven and bake an additional 15 minutes. **Yield:** 8-10 servings.

BEEF BISCUITS

Carolyn Pauling, Paullina, Iowa

My 17-year-old granddaughter introduced me to this tasty recipe. She first made it in her home economics class.

  3 **tubes (8 ounces *each*) refrigerated biscuits**
  1 **pound ground beef**
  1 **small onion, chopped**
1/4 **cup chopped green pepper**
  1 **can (8 ounces) tomato sauce**
  1 **teaspoon salt**
1/2 **teaspoon pepper**
1/2 **teaspoon dried oregano**
Cooking oil

On a floured surface, roll each biscuit into a 5-in. circle; set aside. Brown beef, onion and green pepper; drain. Stir in tomato sauce, salt, pepper and oregano; mix well. Place 1 rounded tablespoonful of meat mixture onto each biscuit. Fold in half and press firmly with the tines of a fork to seal edges. Heat about 3 in. of oil to 375° in a deep fryer. Fry each biscuit until golden brown; drain on paper towels. Serve warm. **Yield:** 24 servings.

▪ ▪ ▪

COUNTRY HAMBURGER PIE
Melissa Brown, Mansfield, Pennsylvania

This all-in-one country dinner is fast and easy to prepare. Those are important qualities after a full day of chores!

CRUST:
- 1 pound lean ground beef
- 1/2 cup tomato sauce
- 1/2 cup dry bread crumbs
- 1/4 cup chopped onion
- 1/2 teaspoon salt
- 1/2 teaspoon pepper
- 1/4 cup chopped green pepper
- 1/2 teaspoon dried oregano

FILLING:
- 1-1/2 cups tomato sauce
- 1-1/3 cups uncooked instant rice
- 1 cup water
- 1/4 teaspoon salt
- 1 cup (4 ounces) shredded cheddar cheese, *divided*

Combine all crust ingredients in a large mixing bowl; mix well. Press the mixture in the bottom and up the sides of a 9-in. pie pan. For filling, combine tomato sauce, rice, water, salt and 3/4 cup cheddar cheese. Spoon into ground beef crust. Cover lightly with foil and bake at 350° for 25 minutes. Remove foil; sprinkle with remaining cheese and bake 3-5 minutes longer or until cheese is melted. **Yield: 6 servings.**

▪ ▪ ▪

ITALIAN VEGETABLE HOT DISH
Judy Wulf, Hancock, Minnesota

This dish became a favorite in our home for two reasons: Everyone, including our children, loves the Italian flavor... plus, it's a great way to get kids to eat their vegetables without complaining!

CRUST:
- 2-2/3 cups all-purpose flour
- 3/4 teaspoon salt
- 1 cup butter *or* margarine
- 1/2 cup ice water

FILLING:
- 1-1/2 pounds ground beef
- 1 medium onion, chopped
- 1-1/2 teaspoons salt
- 1 teaspoon pepper
- 2 cans (10-3/4 ounces *each*) condensed tomato soup, undiluted
- 1 package (1-1/2 ounces) spaghetti sauce mix
- 4 cups sliced cooked carrots
- 4 cups cut cooked green beans
- 3 cups (12 ounces) shredded mozzarella cheese

For crust, combine flour and salt in a mixing bowl. Cut in butter until mixture resembles coarse meal. Add ice water; mix until dough forms a ball. Divide dough in half. Roll out one piece into a 13-in. x 9-in. rectangle; place in the bottom of a 13-in. x 9-in. x 2-in. baking dish. Repeat with remaining piece of dough; set aside. For filling, brown ground beef, onion, salt and pepper in a skillet; drain. Stir in soup, spaghetti sauce mix, carrots and green beans. Spoon over bottom crust. Sprinkle with cheese. Cover with remaining dough. Bake at 350° for 80-90 minutes or until bubbly and golden brown. **Yield: 10-12 servings.**

▪ ▪ ▪

MEAT-AND-POTATO QUICHE
Esther Beachy, Hutchinson, Kansas

This hearty dish is welcome anytime, of course...but our family especially enjoys it at breakfast! It just seems to get the day off to an extra-good start.

- 3 tablespoons vegetable oil
- 3 cups shredded peeled potatoes, well drained
- 1 cup (4 ounces) shredded mozzarella cheese
- 3/4 cup browned ground beef
- 1/4 cup chopped onion
- 1 cup heavy cream
- 5 eggs
- 1/2 teaspoon salt
- 1/8 teaspoon pepper
- 1 tablespoon minced fresh parsley

Combine oil and potatoes in a 10-in. pie plate. Press mixture down evenly to form a crust. Bake at 425° for 10 minutes or until lightly browned. Remove from oven and layer with mozzarella, ground beef and onion. Beat together cream, eggs, salt and pepper; pour over beef mixture. Sprinkle with parsley. Bake for 30 minutes or until a knife inserted in center comes out clean. **Yield: 4-6 servings.**

▪ ▪ ▪

BEEF AND CABBAGE PIE
Mary Lou Smarsh, Laurel, Montana

I especially like to make this when I can use fresh potatoes and cabbage from my garden. It's mmm-good!

- 1-1/2 cups shredded peeled potatoes
- 1-1/2 cups (6 ounces) shredded cheddar cheese, *divided*
- 1/2 teaspoon pepper, *divided*
- 1/4 teaspoon onion salt, *divided*
- 1 pound ground beef
- 1-1/2 cups shredded cabbage
- 1 can (4 ounces) chopped green chilies, drained
- 1/2 cup bottled taco sauce

Additional taco sauce, optional

In a large mixing bowl, combine potatoes, 1/2 cup cheese, 1/4 teaspoon pepper and 1/8 teaspoon onion salt. Press into the bottom and up the sides of a greased 10-in. pie plate. Bake at 350° for 20 minutes. Meanwhile, in a large skillet, brown ground beef; drain. Add cabbage; saute over high heat for 2-3 minutes or until crisp. Remove from heat. Stir in chilies, taco sauce and remaining pepper and onion salt. Mix well. Spoon into potato crust; bake another 20 minutes. Remove from oven and sprinkle with remaining cheese. Bake 2-3 minutes longer or until the cheese is melted. Let stand 10 minutes before serving. Serve with additional taco sauce if desired. **Yield: 6 servings.**

two ungreased baking sheets. Bake at 400° for 20-25 minutes or until golden brown. **Yield:** 8 pasties.

■ ■ ■

CHEESEBURGER QUICHE

Pauline Schuurman, Tillsonburg, Ontario
(PICTURED AT LEFT)

Besides being delicious, this dish is easy to make with on-hand ingredients—I don't have to run to the grocer first!

- 1/2 pound ground beef
- 1/3 cup chopped onion
- 1/2 cup mayonnaise
- 1/2 cup milk
- 1/8 teaspoon dried oregano
- 1/2 teaspoon salt
- 1/8 teaspoon pepper
- 3 eggs, beaten
- 1-1/2 cups (6 ounces) shredded cheddar cheese, *divided*
- 1 unbaked pie shell (9 inches)

In a skillet, brown ground beef and onion; drain and set aside. In a mixing bowl, combine mayonnaise, milk, oregano, salt and pepper; beat in eggs. Stir in beef mixture and 1 cup cheese. Pour into pie shell. Bake at 350° for 35-40 minutes or until set. Remove from oven and sprinkle with remaining cheese. Allow to stand 5 minutes before cutting. **Yield:** 6 servings.

■ ■ ■

CORNISH PASTIES

Judy Marsden, Ontario, California
(PICTURED AT LEFT)

These are a bit different from traditional pasties, but the ingredients are probably already on your pantry shelf. My husband really enjoys these, so I like to double the recipe and freeze the extras to have on hand as a quick meal.

- 1/2 pound ground beef
- 2 tablespoons all-purpose flour
- 1/2 to 1 teaspoon seasoned salt
- 1 tablespoon chopped fresh parsley
- 1 teaspoon instant beef bouillon granules
- 1/4 cup water
- 1 cup diced peeled potatoes
- 1/2 cup diced carrots
- 2 tablespoons finely chopped onion
- 2 packages (11 ounces *each*) pie crust mix

Water

In a skillet, brown ground beef; drain well. Add flour, seasoned salt and parsley; stir until well coated. Dissolve bouillon in water; stir into meat mixture. Add potatoes, carrots and onion. Cover and cook over medium heat until vegetables are crisp-tender. Cool. Meanwhile, prepare pie crusts according to package directions. On a floured surface, roll each pie crust mixture into a 12-in. square. Cut each square into four 6-in. squares. Place about 1/3 cup of meat mixture in center of each square. Moisten edges of pastry with water and fold over meat mixture to form a triangle. Press the edges with a fork to seal. Make a 1-in. slit in the top of each triangle. Place on

> **FRESH FROM THE OVEN.** Pictured at left from top to bottom: Cheeseburger Quiche and Cornish Pasties (both recipes above).

■ ■ ■

UPSIDE-DOWN MEAT PIE

Cora Dowling, Toledo, Ohio

This recipe, which my sister gave me more than 30 years ago, is perfect whenever friends drop by—it mixes up in a jiffy, yet it's substantial and satisfying.

- 1 pound ground beef
- 1/2 cup chopped onion
- 1/2 teaspoon salt
- 1 can (15 ounces) tomato sauce

BAKING POWDER BISCUITS:
- 1 cup all-purpose flour
- 2 teaspoons baking powder
- 1 teaspoon celery salt
- 1 teaspoon paprika
- 1/2 teaspoon salt
- 1/4 teaspoon pepper
- 3 tablespoons butter *or* margarine
- 1/2 cup milk

In a large skillet, cook ground beef and onion until the beef is browned and onion is tender; drain. Add salt and tomato sauce; simmer 10-15 minutes. Spoon mixture into a 2-qt. casserole; set aside. For biscuits, combine flour, baking powder, celery salt, paprika, salt and pepper in a mixing bowl. Cut in butter until mixture resembles coarse meal. Add milk and stir until a soft dough forms. Drop by tablespoonfuls onto meat mixture. Bake, uncovered, at 475° for 20 minutes or until biscuits are golden. **Yield:** 4 servings.

■ ■ ■

ZUCCHINI PIZZA

Lila McNamara, Dickinson, North Dakota

When zucchini is plentiful in late summer, I keep this recipe at the front of my card file. It's a wonderful way to take advantage of the season's bounty—and feed a crowd!

- 4 cups shredded peeled zucchini, drained and squeezed dry
- 2 cups cooked rice
- 1-1/2 cups (6 ounces) shredded mozzarella cheese
- 1 cup grated Parmesan cheese
- 2 eggs
- 1 pound ground beef
- 1 medium onion, chopped
- 1-1/2 cups prepared spaghetti sauce
- 1 teaspoon dried oregano
- 1/2 teaspoon salt
- 2 cups (8 ounces) shredded cheddar cheese

In a mixing bowl, combine zucchini, rice, mozzarella cheese, Parmesan cheese and eggs until well blended. Press mixture into a greased 15-in. x 11-in. x 1-in. baking pan. Bake at 400° for 20-25 minutes or until the crust is set and lightly browned. Meanwhile, brown ground beef and onion; drain. Stir in spaghetti sauce, oregano and salt. Mix well. Spoon beef mixture over zucchini crust. Sprinkle with cheddar cheese. Bake at 400° for 15 minutes. Let stand 5 minutes before serving. **Yield:** 12-15 servings.

■ ■ ■

TOPSY-TURVY PIE

Kara Kimberline, Galion, Ohio

I've enjoyed this since I was a little girl, when my mother used to make it. It's both filling and flavorful.

        1 pound ground beef
    1/2 cup chopped onion
    1/4 cup chopped green pepper
        1 can (8 ounces) tomato sauce
        1 can (4-1/2 ounces) chopped ripe olives, drained
    1/2 teaspoon salt
        1 teaspoon chili powder
BISCUIT TOPPING:
        1 cup buttermilk biscuit mix
    1/4 cup milk
        2 tablespoons butter *or* margarine, melted

In a skillet, cook ground beef, onion and green pepper until beef is browned and onion is tender; drain. Stir in tomato sauce, olives, salt and chili powder; mix well. Pour into a 9-in. pie plate; set aside. For topping, combine biscuit mix, milk and butter in a mixing bowl; beat 15 strokes. Turn onto a floured surface and knead 8-10 times. Roll into a 10-in. circle. Place over meat mixture; crimp edges to seal. Cut small slits in crust to vent steam. Bake at 425° for 15-20 minutes. Remove from oven and let stand a few minutes. Invert onto a serving plate. Cut into wedges to serve. **Yield:** 4-6 servings.

■ ■ ■

DIFFERENT PIZZA

Carla Wiese, Ripon, Wisconsin

"Different" can be delicious! We often have this as our Sunday-evening supper, and everyone raves about it—including our teenage son.

TOPPING:
        1 pound ground beef
    1/3 cup chopped onion
        2 teaspoons Worcestershire sauce
    1/2 teaspoon dried marjoram
    1/2 teaspoon dried oregano
    1/4 teaspoon dried sage
    1/4 teaspoon pepper
        1 can (10-3/4 ounces) condensed cream of mushroom soup, undiluted
CRUST:
        2 cups all-purpose flour
    1/2 teaspoon salt
        2 teaspoons baking powder
    1/4 cup shortening
        1 cup milk
        2 cups (8 ounces) shredded mozzarella cheese

For topping, lightly brown ground beef and onion in a skillet; drain well. Stir in Worcestershire sauce, marjoram, oregano, sage, pepper and soup. Stir until well blended; set aside. For crust, combine flour, salt and baking powder in a mixing bowl; cut in shortening. Add milk and stir until combined (mixture resembles a soft biscuit dough). Pat dough into a lightly greased 15-in. x 10-in. x 1-in. baking pan. Spread beef mixture over crust. Sprin-

kle with mozzarella cheese. Bake at 400° for 25-30 minutes or until lightly browned. **Yield:** 16 servings.

■ ■ ■

SAUSAGE BREAD

Jan Young, Fort Smith, Arkansas

This beef-and-bread roll is really easy to make. The seasonings give the beef a flavor like sausage, hence its name.

        1 pound lean ground beef
    1/2 teaspoon dried oregano
    1/2 teaspoon garlic powder
    1/2 teaspoon salt
    1/4 teaspoon crushed red pepper flakes
    1/4 teaspoon dried sage
        2 eggs, lightly beaten
        1 cup (4 ounces) shredded cheddar cheese
    1/2 cup grated Parmesan cheese
        1 loaf frozen bread dough, thawed
        1 tablespoon butter *or* margarine, melted

In a mixing bowl, combine ground beef, oregano, garlic powder, salt, red pepper flakes, sage, eggs and cheeses; mix well and set aside. On a floured surface, roll bread dough into a 12-in. x 10-in. rectangle. Spread meat mixture to within 1 in. of the edges. Roll the rectangle, jelly-roll style, starting at narrow end. Pinch the ends and bottom seam to seal. Place seam side down on an ungreased baking sheet. Place in a warm place and let rise about 1/2 hour. Bake at 350° for 30-35 minutes or until golden brown and bread tests done. Brush with butter before serving. **Yield:** 8-10 servings.

■ ■ ■

WAGON WHEEL TURNOVERS

Donna Meyer, New Albin, Iowa

When my children were still at home, I made this often because they loved it. They still do (and so do I!). With a salad or a simple cooked vegetable alongside, these turnovers make a complete meal.

        1 pound ground beef
        1 cup chopped onion
        1 cup fresh mushrooms, sliced
        1 can (11 ounces) condensed cheese soup, undiluted
    1/4 teaspoon poultry seasoning
        2 cups all-purpose flour
        2 teaspoons baking powder
    1/2 teaspoon salt
    1/2 teaspoon curry powder
    1/3 cup butter *or* margarine
        1 can (8 ounces) tomato sauce, *divided*
    1/3 cup water
        1 egg white, beaten
    1/2 cup milk

In a skillet, brown ground beef with onion and mushrooms; drain. Stir in 1/3 cup cheese soup and poultry seasoning. Set aside to cool. In a mixing bowl, combine flour, baking powder, salt and curry powder. Cut in butter until mixture resembles fine meal. Stir in 1/3 cup tomato sauce and water. Knead on a floured surface until a soft dough forms. Roll into a 14-in. square. Cut into four 7-

in. squares. Divide meat mixture evenly among the squares. Fold dough over meat mixture to form a triangle; pinch edges to seal. Place on a baking sheet and brush each turnover lightly with egg white. Bake at 400° for 20 minutes or until lightly browned. In a small saucepan, combine milk, remaining tomato sauce and cheese soup; heat through. Serve over turnovers. **Yield:** 4 servings.

■ ■ ■

FRENCH MEAT PIE

Rita Winterberger, Huson, Montana
(PICTURED ON COVER)

Some time ago, a co-worker brought a meat pie to lunch. The aroma was familiar—and after one taste, I was amazed to discover it was the same pie my grandmother used to serve when I was a youngster! She shared the recipe, and I have been enjoying it ever since.

2 tablespoons cooking oil
1 large onion, thinly sliced
1 pound ground beef
1 pound ground pork
1 cup mashed potatoes
1 can (8 ounces) mixed vegetables, drained
2 teaspoons ground allspice
1 teaspoon salt
1/4 teaspoon pepper
Pastry for double-crust pie (9 inches)
1 egg, beaten, optional

In a skillet, heat oil over medium. Saute onion until tender. Remove and set aside. Brown beef and pork together; drain. Combine onion, meat, potatoes, vegetables and seasonings. Line pie plate with pastry; fill with meat mixture. Top with crust; seal and flute edges. Make slits in top crust. Brush with egg if desired. Bake at 375° for 30-35 minutes or until golden brown. **Yield:** 6-8 servings.

■ ■ ■

CRAZY CRUST PIZZA

Cynthia Mason, Wamego, Kansas

The crust adds its own savory flavor to this pizza. Don't expect any leftovers—it's that good!

1-1/2 pounds ground beef
1 cup all-purpose flour
Dash salt and pepper
1 teaspoon Italian seasoning
2 eggs
2/3 cup milk
1/4 cup chopped onion
1 can (4 ounces) sliced mushrooms, drained
1 can (8 ounces) pizza sauce
1 cup (4 ounces) shredded mozzarella cheese

In a skillet, brown beef; drain and set aside. In a small bowl, combine flour, salt, pepper, Italian seasoning, eggs and milk; beat until smooth. Pour batter into a greased and floured 12-in. or 14-in. pizza pan. Spoon beef, onion and mushrooms over batter. Bake at 425° for 25-30 minutes. Remove from oven. Top with pizza sauce and sprinkle with mozzarella cheese. Return to oven and bake 10-15 minutes longer. **Yield:** 4-6 servings.

■ ■ ■

BEEF PASTRY POCKETS

Andrea Chaput, Blaine, Washington

My husband and I raise beef cattle on our farm—that's why I'm always on the lookout for tasty recipes like this one.

3/4 pound ground beef
1-1/2 cups (6 ounces) shredded cheddar cheese
3/4 cup cottage cheese
2 eggs, lightly beaten
1/2 teaspoon pepper
1 box (17-1/4 ounces) frozen puff pastry, thawed

In a large skillet, brown beef; drain well and allow to cool. Add cheddar cheese, cottage cheese, eggs and pepper; mix well. Cut pastry into eight 5-in. squares, 1/4-in. thick. Place heaping 1/3 cupfuls of meat/cheese mixture in center of squares, folding over one edge to form a triangle. Moisten edges with water; press together with a fork to seal. Place on an ungreased baking sheet; bake at 400° for 20 minutes or until golden brown. **Yield:** 8 servings.

■ ■ ■

STUFFED PIZZA

Michelle Martin, Niceville, Florida

This is really more than just a pizza—it's a hearty, stick-to-your-ribs feast!

CRUST:
1 tablespoon sugar
2 packages (1/4 ounce *each*) active dry yeast
1-1/4 cups warm water (105° to 115°)
3-1/4 cups all-purpose flour
1 tablespoon salt
1/4 cup vegetable oil
MEAT FILLING:
1 pound ground beef
1 medium onion, chopped
1 can (2-1/4 ounces) sliced ripe olives, drained
1 can (4 ounces) sliced mushrooms, drained
1 package (10 ounces) frozen chopped spinach, thawed and well drained
2 cups (8 ounces) shredded mozzarella cheese
1 jar (32 ounces) spaghetti sauce

For crust, dissolve sugar and yeast in water; set aside. In a large mixing bowl, combine flour and salt. Stir in yeast mixture and oil; mix until dough forms a ball. Knead on a lightly floured surface 6-8 minutes or until smooth. Place in a greased bowl, turning once to grease top. Cover and let rise in a warm place until doubled, about 1 hour. Meanwhile, for filling, brown ground beef and onion in a skillet; drain and cool. Stir in olives, mushrooms, spinach and cheese; set aside. Punch dough down. Divide into two pieces, one slightly larger than the other. Roll out the larger piece into a 15-in. circle. Press into the bottom and up the sides of a greased 12-in. deep-dish pizza pan. Cover with meat mixture. Roll out remaining dough into a 12-in. circle; place over meat mixture. Crimp edges of crusts together to seal; gently press top crust onto meat filling. Cut a 1-in. slit in center of crust. Spread spaghetti sauce over top crust. Bake at 475° for 35-40 minutes or until lightly browned. **Yield:** 10-12 servings.

Skillet Suppers

■ ■ ■

SWEET-AND-SOUR MEATBALLS

Cathy MacPherson, Prescott, Ontario
(PICTURED AT LEFT)

We raise our own beef cattle, so there's always plenty of ground beef on hand. I enjoy preparing this dish, because I know there will be no leftovers. Plus, these meatballs are as attractive as they are delicious.

      1 egg, beaten
  1/4 cup milk
  1/2 cup dry bread crumbs
      2 tablespoons finely chopped onion
  3/4 teaspoon salt
  1/2 teaspoon Worcestershire sauce
      1 pound lean ground beef
SAUCE:
  1/2 cup packed brown sugar
      2 tablespoons cornstarch
      1 can (20 ounces) pineapple chunks with juice
  1/3 cup vinegar
      1 tablespoon soy sauce
      1 medium green pepper, cut into bite-size pieces

Mix together first six ingredients; add beef and mix well. Shape into 1-1/2-in. balls. In a skillet, brown meatballs on all sides, turning often; remove and set aside. Drain fat. For sauce, combine brown sugar and cornstarch in the skillet. Stir in pineapple with juice, vinegar and soy sauce. Bring to a boil, stirring constantly. Reduce heat; cover and simmer for about 10 minutes or until sauce thickens, stirring occasionally. Add green pepper; cover and simmer until tender, about 5 minutes. Return meatballs to skillet and heat through. **Yield:** 4-6 servings.

■ ■ ■

HAMBURGER STROGANOFF

Jutta Doering, Kelowna, British Columbia
(PICTURED AT LEFT)

I just love cooking with ground beef, especially when the result is a rib-sticking and economical dish like this. I serve it over poppy seed noodles for extra flavor.

  1-1/2 pounds lean ground beef
    1/2 cup chopped onion
        2 tablespoons butter *or* margarine
        2 tablespoons all-purpose flour
    1/2 teaspoon salt
        1 garlic clove, minced

DELUXE DINNERS. Pictured at left, clockwise from bottom: Spaghetti Squash with Meat Sauce, Sweet-and-Sour Meatballs and Hamburger Stroganoff (all recipes on this page).

  1/4 teaspoon pepper
      1 can (4 ounces) mushroom pieces and stems, drained
      1 can (10-3/4 ounces) condensed cream of chicken soup, undiluted
      1 cup (8 ounces) sour cream
POPPY SEED NOODLES:
      8 ounces wide noodles, cooked and drained
      2 teaspoons poppy seed
      1 tablespoon butter *or* margarine, melted
Chopped fresh parsley

In a skillet, cook ground beef and onion in butter until the beef is browned and the onion is tender. Stir in flour, salt, garlic, pepper and mushrooms. Cook for 5 minutes, stirring constantly. Stir in soup; bring to a boil, stirring constantly. Reduce heat; simmer, uncovered, for 10 minutes, stirring occasionally. Stir in sour cream; heat through, but do not boil. Meanwhile, combine noodles, poppy seed and butter; toss lighly. Spoon stroganoff over noodles. Garnish with parsley. **Yield:** 6 servings.

■ ■ ■

SPAGHETTI SQUASH WITH MEAT SAUCE

Lina Vainauskas, Shaw Air Force Base, South Carolina
(PICTURED AT LEFT)

Neither my mother nor I had tried spaghetti squash before, so when we cooked this recipe together, all we could do was grin and say, "Wow!" It's fun to separate the noodle-like strands from the squash shell, but the eating is the best part!

        1 medium spaghetti squash (about 8 inches)
        1 cup water
        1 pound ground beef
        1 large onion, chopped
        1 medium green pepper, chopped
        1 teaspoon garlic powder
        2 teaspoons dried basil
  1-1/2 teaspoons dried oregano
        1 teaspoon salt
    1/2 teaspoon pepper
  1/4 to 1/2 teaspoon chili powder
        1 can (28 ounces) tomato puree
        1 cup grated Parmesan cheese, *divided*

Slice the squash lengthwise and scoop out seeds. Place squash, cut side down, in a baking dish. Add water and cover tightly with foil. Bake at 375° for 20-30 minutes or until easily pierced with a fork. Meanwhile, brown beef in a large skillet; drain. Add onion, green pepper, herbs and seasonings; saute until onion is transparent. Stir in tomato puree. Cover and cook over low heat, stirring occasionally. Scoop out the squash, separating the strands with a fork. Just before serving; stir 1/2 cup Parmesan cheese into the meat sauce. Serve sauce over spaghetti squash and pass remaining Parmesan. **Yield:** 6 servings.

ITALIAN SPAGHETTI AND MEATBALLS

Etta Winter, Pavilion, New York
(PICTURED ON COVER)

This is an authentic Italian recipe. It was given to me by my cousin's wife, who is from Italy. It's so hearty and satisfying, everyone's eyes light up when I tell my family that we're having this for supper!

　2 cans (28 ounces *each*) tomatoes with liquid, cut up
　1 can (12 ounces) tomato paste
1-1/2 cups water, *divided*
　1 tablespoon sugar
1-1/2 teaspoons onion juice
　2 garlic cloves, minced, *divided*
1-1/2 teaspoons dried oregano
2-1/2 teaspoons salt, *divided*
　3/4 teaspoon pepper, *divided*
　1 bay leaf
　6 slices dry bread, torn into pieces
　1 pound ground beef
　2 eggs, beaten
1/2 cup grated Parmesan cheese
　2 tablespoons snipped fresh parsley
　1 to 2 tablespoons cooking oil
Cooked spaghetti
Additional Parmesan cheese, optional

In a large kettle or Dutch oven, combine tomatoes, tomato paste, 1 cup water, sugar, onion juice, 1 garlic clove, oregano, 1-1/2 teaspoons salt, 1/2 teaspoon pepper and the bay leaf. Bring to a boil. Reduce heat and simmer, uncovered, for about 1 hour. Meanwhile, soak bread in remaining water. Squeeze out excess moisture. In a mixing bowl, combine bread with beef, eggs, Parmesan cheese, parsley and remaining garlic, salt and pepper. Shape into 18 meatballs, about 1-1/2-in. diameter. Heat oil in a skillet; brown meatballs slowly over medium heat. Drain; add meatballs to spaghetti sauce. Simmer, uncovered, for 1 hour, stirring occasionally. Remove bay leaf. Serve over spaghetti with additional Parmesan if desired. **Yield:** 6 servings.

TACO-STUFFED POTATOES

Beverly Hockel, Odin, Minnesota

Here's a tasty, different way to serve up the flavor of tacos without having to make a trip to the grocery store for the taco shells. And if you can bake the potatoes in a microwave oven, the whole entree takes only a few minutes to prepare.

　6 medium baking potatoes
　1 pound ground beef
1/2 cup chopped onion
　1 teaspoon chili powder
　1 package (1-1/4 ounces) taco seasoning
3/4 cup water
　1 can (15 ounces) refried beans
　1 cup (4 ounces) shredded cheddar cheese
Sour cream

Bake potatoes in a microwave or conventional oven. Meanwhile, in a skillet, brown ground beef; drain.

Add onion, chili powder, taco seasoning and water. Simmer for 5-10 minutes. Heat refried beans in a small saucepan. Slice baked potatoes open. Spoon taco filling into each; top with 1-2 tablespoons beans and sprinkle with cheese. Microwave for 1 minute. Top with sour cream. **Yield:** 6 servings.

POACHED MEATBALLS IN LEMON SAUCE

Taj Renee Brown, San Antonio, Texas

I discovered this among my collection of Southern recipes, and when I fixed these meatballs for my husband, there wasn't one left! The lemon sauce gives a nice tang to the taste buds.

1/2 cup seasoned dry bread crumbs
　1 egg, beaten
1/2 teaspoon salt
　1 teaspoon grated lemon peel
　1 pound ground beef
2-1/4 cups water, *divided*
　2 beef bouillon cubes
　2 teaspoons cornstarch
　2 tablespoons fresh lemon juice
　2 egg yolks
Cooked rice

In a mixing bowl, combine bread crumbs, egg, salt and lemon peel. Add ground beef; mix well. Shape into 12 meatballs, about 1-1/2 in. in diameter; set aside. In a saucepan, bring 2 cups water to a boil; add bouillon and stir to dissolve. Gently drop meatballs into broth. Reduce heat and simmer for 10 minutes or until the meatballs are no longer pink; remove to a warm bowl. Combine cornstarch and remaining water; stir into broth. Add lemon juice; cook and stir until thickened. Stir a small amount of broth into egg yolks; blend well. Return to saucepan and heat through. Serve sauce over meatballs. **Yield:** 4 servings.

SERBIAN STUFFED CABBAGE

Mrs. Arthur Wahlberg, Goetzville, Michigan

This recipe was given to me by a farmer neighbor. She grew up in a Serbian neighborhood, and said the Serbian name for this dish is Sarma. I always think of this kind lady whenever I make this dish...she and her husband always had a huge garden (one year, they grew five different types of leaf lettuce!), and they were always very generous with their harvests.

　1 pound ground beef
　1 large onion, chopped
　1 medium cabbage (about 3 pounds), cored
1/4 cup uncooked long grain rice
　1 teaspoon salt
1/4 teaspoon pepper
　1 can (8 ounces) sauerkraut, undrained
GRAVY:
　2 tablespoons vegetable oil
　2 tablespoons all-purpose flour
1-1/2 cups water
　2 tablespoons paprika
　1 can (8 ounces) tomato sauce

1 teaspoon salt
1/2 teaspoon pepper

In a skillet, brown beef and onion; drain and set aside. In a Dutch oven or large kettle, bring 2 qts. of water to a boil. Add cabbage; simmer 6-8 minutes. Remove wilted cabbage leaves with a fork; drain and cool. Meanwhile, in a saucepan, add rice to 2 cups boiling water; when water comes to a boil again, remove from the heat. Drain and rinse. Add rice to beef; season with salt and pepper. Remove the large vein from 12 large cabbage leaves. Line bottom of another large kettle with half of the remaining small cabbage leaves; cover with half of the sauerkraut. Place 1 tablespoon of meat mixture on each large cabbage leaf. Fold sides over and roll leaf up tightly lengthwise; tuck loose ends under and place seam side down on top of sauerkraut. Repeat with remaining large leaves and meat mixture. Cover with remaining sauerkraut and small cabbage leaves. For gravy, combine the oil and flour in a small saucepan. Add remaining ingredients and cook over medium heat until slightly thickened; pour over cabbage leaves. Simmer gently over low heat for 1-1/2 to 2 hours, shaking kettle occasionally to prevent sticking. **Yield:** 6 servings.

BAKED POTATOES WITH CHILI
Nadine Behrend, Everett, Washington

To devise this recipe, I just experimented with ingredients that I had on hand—and was delighted with the results! It can easily be doubled to serve more people. And except for the wonderful taste, the best part is that it's a "meal in a spud"...you don't even need a side dish!

4 large baking potatoes
1/2 pound ground beef
1 small zucchini, diced
1/2 cup chopped onion
1 can (16 ounces) chili
Butter, optional
1 cup (4 ounces) shredded cheddar cheese
Sour cream
Salsa

Bake potatoes in a microwave or conventional oven. In a skillet, brown ground beef; drain. Add onion and zucchini; saute until onion is transparent. Heat chili in a saucepan; stir in ground beef and vegetables. Slice baked potatoes open; add a pat of butter if desired. Spoon chili into each potato and top with cheese, sour cream and salsa. **Yield:** 4 servings.

BEEF FRIED RICE
Cathy Wadden, Hamilton, Ontario

I came up with this recipe by experimenting—and it's become a family favorite. I often add whatever vegetables and seasonings I have on hand.

1-1/2 pounds ground beef
2 garlic cloves, minced
1 cup finely chopped carrots
1 cup finely chopped celery
1/2 cup finely chopped onion
3/4 cup chopped fresh mushrooms
1/2 cup frozen peas, thawed
1 tablespoon dried parsley flakes
1 teaspoon dried basil
1/4 teaspoon ground ginger
Salt and pepper to taste
5 cups cooked long grain rice
2 eggs, scrambled
1/4 to 1/2 cup soy sauce

In a large skillet, brown beef. Drain all but 2-3 tablespoons fat. Stir-fry garlic, carrots, celery and onion. Add mushrooms and peas; cook until all vegetables are tender. Add parsley, basil, ginger, salt, pepper, rice and eggs; stir until well mixed. Add soy sauce and heat through. **Yield:** 8-10 servings.

CURLY NOODLE DINNER
Gwen Clemon, Soldier, Iowa

The calendar on my kitchen wall is often busy with church work, 4-H leader meetings and the school activities of our three daughters...so this recipe is perfect for our busy family. I just add fruit or raw vegetables for a complete meal in just a few minutes.

1 pound ground beef
1 package (3 ounces) beef-flavored Oriental Ramen noodles
1 can (14-1/2 ounces) stewed tomatoes
1 can (8-1/2 ounces) whole kernel corn, drained

In a skillet, brown beef; drain. Stir in noodles with contents of accompanying seasoning packet, tomatoes and corn; mix well. Bring to a boil. Reduce heat; cover and simmer for 10 minutes or until the noodles are tender. **Yield:** 4-6 servings.

CHOP SUEY
Debra Weihert, Waterloo, Wisconsin

This recipe is my children's all-time favorite meal. How much do they like it? Even more than they like pizza...and that's a lot!

1 pound ground beef
2 beef bouillon cubes
2 cups water, *divided*
2 tablespoons cornstarch
1 can (28 ounces) chop suey vegetables, drained
2 tablespoons soy sauce
Cooked rice
Chow mein noodles

In a skillet, brown beef; drain. Dissolve bouillon in 1-1/2 cups boiling water; add to skillet. Combine remaining water with cornstarch; stir into beef mixture. Bring to a boil; reduce heat and simmer until thickened. Add vegetables and soy sauce; stir and cook until heated through, about 15 minutes. Serve over rice; sprinkle with chow mein noodles. **Yield:** 4-6 servings.

SIZZLING SENSATIONS. Clockwise from top left: Lentil Stew (p. 74), East-West Stir-Fry (p. 74), Spanish Rice (p. 74), Okie Beans (p. 74) and Aunt Fran's Goulash (p. 75).

and steam for 1 minute. Mix in spinach. Serve immediately over rice. **Yield:** 4 servings.

■ ■ ■

Spanish Rice

Beverly Austin, Fulton, Missouri
(PICTURED ON PAGE 73)

I don't know the origin of this recipe, but it's one that has been in my family for a long time. I can remember eating it often as a little girl.

   1 pound ground beef
   1 cup chopped onion
1/2 cup chopped green pepper
   1 garlic clove, minced
   1 tablespoon chili powder
   1 bottle (32 ounces) tomato *or* vegetable juice
   1 cup uncooked long grain rice
1/2 teaspoon salt

In a skillet, brown ground beef; drain. Stir in the onion, green pepper, garlic and chili powder. Cook and stir until the vegetables are tender. Stir in remaining ingredients; bring to a boil. Reduce heat; cover and simmer for 20-25 minutes or until the rice is tender and most of the liquid is absorbed. **Yield:** 6-8 servings.

■ ■ ■

Western Hash

Karen Ann Bland, Gove, Kansas

Believe it or not, I originally heard this recipe on a television commercial! That was many years ago, and I still make this hash often. Try it with some corn bread or corn chips on the side.

   1 pound ground beef
   1 can (28 ounces) tomatoes with liquid, cut up
   1 cup uncooked long grain rice
   1 cup chopped green pepper
1/2 cup chopped onion
   1 teaspoon salt
1/2 teaspoon dried basil
1/4 teaspoon pepper
1/2 pound sliced process cheese *or* 1-1/2 cups (6 ounces) shredded cheddar cheese

In a skillet, brown beef; drain. Stir in tomatoes, rice, green pepper, onion and seasonings; mix well. Cover and simmer about 30 minutes. Top with cheese slices or shredded cheddar; cook until cheese melts. **Yield:** 6-8 servings.

■ ■ ■

Okie Beans

Linda Creason, McAlester, Oklahoma
(PICTURED ON PAGE 73)

I got the original version of this recipe from a pastor's wife. That makes sense—because it makes up a generous potful that's perfect for our church suppers.

1-1/2 pounds ground beef
   1 medium onion, chopped
   1 pound smoked sausage, cut into 1/2-inch slices
   1 cup cubed fully cooked ham

■ ■ ■

Lentil Stew

Carol Wolfer, Lebanon, Oregon
(PICTURED ON PAGE 72)

This hearty stew is a favorite with our family, along with a basket of my homemade breadsticks. Since lentils don't require the long soaking time that dried beans do, you can begin making this dish just an hour before supper—not the night before!

   1 cup dry lentils
2-1/2 cups water
   2 beef bouillon cubes
1/2 pound ground beef, browned and drained
   2 carrots, sliced
   2 cups tomato juice
1/2 teaspoon dried oregano
1/2 cup chopped onion
   2 celery stalks, chopped
   1 garlic clove, minced

Clean and rinse lentils. In a saucepan, bring lentils, water and bouillon to a boil. Reduce heat and simmer, uncovered, about 20 minutes. Stir in remaining ingredients. Return to a boil; reduce heat and simmer 20-30 minutes longer or until the vegetables are tender. **Yield:** 6 servings.

■ ■ ■

East-West Stir-Fry

Nan Radabaugh, Perrysburg, Ohio
(PICTURED ON PAGE 73)

This makes a pretty, colorful meal. For a different taste, try serving a stir-fry over baked or mashed potatoes—that's how I sometimes serve this dish.

   1 pound lean ground beef
   3 tablespoons peanut *or* vegetable oil, *divided*
   1 medium onion, cut into wedges
1/2 cup diagonally sliced celery
   1 medium carrot, peeled and cut in paper-thin strips
1/4 pound fresh green beans, sliced lengthwise
   1 can (8 ounces) sliced water chestnuts, drained
   4 large fresh mushrooms, thinly sliced
1/2 cup chicken broth
   1 tablespoon honey
   2 tablespoons soy sauce
   1 tablespoon cornstarch
   2 tablespoons water
   8 to 10 ounces fresh spinach
   3 cups cooked rice

On waxed paper, shape the ground beef into a 7-in. square. Using a large knife, cut beef into 1-in. cubes. Heat 1 tablespoon oil in a skillet over high heat; add half of the beef cubes. Stir-fry about 3 minutes or until no pink remains. Remove beef and keep warm; repeat with remaining beef cubes. Heat remaining oil in skillet; stir-fry onion, celery, carrot, beans, water chestnuts and mushrooms for 2 minutes. Add broth; reduce heat. Cover and steam for 2-3 minutes, stirring occasionally. Stir in honey and soy sauce. Dissolve cornstarch in water; add to skillet. Return meat to skillet. Place spinach on top of meat/vegetable mixture; cover

1 cup packed brown sugar
2 tablespoons prepared mustard
2 tablespoons vinegar
1 bottle (32 ounces) ketchup
1 can (16 ounces) red kidney beans, undrained
1 can (16 ounces) great northern beans, undrained
1 can (16 ounces) pinto beans, undrained
1 can (16 ounces) butter beans, undrained

In a large skillet or Dutch oven, cook ground beef and onion until the beef is browned and the onion is tender; drain. Add sausage and ham. Combine the brown sugar, mustard, vinegar and ketchup; stir into beef mixture. Add all beans and mix well. Simmer, uncovered, stirring occcasionally, for 2 to 2-1/2 hours or until sauce has thickened. **Yield:** 16-20 servings.

AUNT FRAN'S GOULASH

LaVergne Krones, Matteson, Illinois
(PICTURED ON PAGE 72)

When I was a young girl, Aunt Fran always made this when we went to visit...my brother and I would have been disappointed if she didn't because it was our favorite. It's quick to make on busy days, and also freezes well.

1-1/2 pounds ground beef
1 medium onion, diced
1 can (10-3/4 ounces) condensed tomato soup, undiluted
1 can (8 ounces) tomato sauce
1 can (15 ounces) kidney beans, drained
1 beef bouillon cube
1-1/2 cups water
Dash pepper
8 ounces corkscrew noodles, cooked and drained
Grated Parmesan cheese, optional

In a skillet, brown beef. Drain fat. Add onion and cook until tender, about 5 minutes; set aside. In a large saucepan, combine soup, tomato sauce, beans, bouillon, water and pepper. Add cooked noodles and beef; heat through. If desired, sprinkle Parmesan cheese on top. **Yield:** 4-6 servings.

CAMPER'S SPECIAL

Marie Hart, Fombell, Pennsylvania

When you're on the road, this dish comes in handy—and since my husband and I often enjoy traveling by ourselves, we can usually enjoy leftovers the next day. We live on a small farm and have 4 grown children and 9 grandchildren.

1 pound ground beef
1 medium onion, chopped
3/4 cup ketchup
1 can (16 ounces) baked beans
2 teaspoons prepared mustard
3 cups cubed cooked peeled potatoes
Salt and pepper to taste

In a skillet, brown ground beef with onion until the beef is browned and the onion is tender; drain. Stir in

ketchup, beans and mustard; cook over medium heat until hot and bubbly. Gently stir in potatoes and heat through. Add salt and pepper. **Yield:** 4 servings.

BAKED BEANS OLE'

Kay Townsend, Obion, Tennessee

This dish is a real time-saver for me. My husband is pastor of a small country church and we have two young daughters, so our schedule can get awfully busy!

1/2 pound ground beef
1 cup chopped onion
2 garlic cloves, minced
2 cans (16 ounces *each*) pork and beans
1 cup picante sauce

In a skillet, cook ground beef with onion and garlic until the beef is browned and the onion is tender; drain. Stir in remaining ingredients. Bring to a boil; reduce heat and simmer 10 minutes, stirring occasionally. **Yield:** 6-8 servings.

SPAGHETTI SAUCE

Carol Ulliac, Atmore, Alberta

Chock-full of hearty meat and vegetables, this sauce freezes beautifully—so I serve some on the same day I cook it, then pack the rest in airtight containers and freeze for up to 6 months. It's convenient to have on hand when unexpected company drops in...or whenever your busy day doesn't allow much time for cooking "from scratch"!

2 pounds ground beef
1 large green pepper, chopped
1-1/2 cups chopped celery
1-1/2 cups chopped onion
1 garlic clove, minced
1-1/2 cups chopped carrots
1 can (8 ounces) mushroom pieces and stems, drained
2 cans (10-3/4 ounces *each*) condensed tomato soup, undiluted
1 can (16 ounces) tomatoes with liquid, cut up
1 can (6 ounces) tomato paste
1-1/2 cups water
1 bottle (12 ounces) chili sauce
1 tablespoon Worcestershire sauce
1/8 teaspoon hot pepper sauce
1 tablespoon sugar
1 to 2 tablespoons steak sauce
3 bay leaves
2 teaspoons salt
1 teaspoon pepper
1-1/2 teaspoons dried thyme
1-1/2 teaspoons dried oregano
1-1/2 teaspoons dried sage
1/2 to 1 teaspoon ground allspice

Brown ground beef in a large skillet or Dutch oven; drain. Add green pepper, celery, onion, garlic and carrots; cook and stir until tender. Stir in remaining ingredients; bring to a boil. Reduce heat and simmer, uncovered, for about 3-4 hours, stirring occasionally. **Yield:** 2-1/2 quarts.

MEATBALL STEW

Savilla Zook, Seabrook, Maryland
(PICTURED AT LEFT)

Many years ago, the Farm Journal published a recipe that became the "jumping-off point" for my version. It's as colorful as it is delicious. I often serve it over wide egg noodles or atop steamed rice—but it's also good just as it is.

    1-1/2 pounds lean ground beef
        1 cup soft bread crumbs
      1/4 cup finely chopped onion
        1 egg, beaten
        1 teaspoon salt
      1/2 teaspoon dried marjoram
      1/4 teaspoon dried thyme
        2 tablespoons vegetable oil
        2 cans (10-3/4 ounces *each*) condensed
          tomato soup, undiluted
        2 cans (10-1/2 ounces *each*) condensed beef
          broth, undiluted
        4 medium potatoes, peeled and diced
        4 carrots, diced
        1 jar (16 ounces) whole onions, drained
      1/4 cup minced fresh parsley

In a mixing bowl, combine the ground beef, bread crumbs, onion, egg, salt, marjoram and thyme; mix well. Shape into 24 meatballs. Heat oil in a Dutch oven. Brown meatballs; drain. Add soup, beef broth, potatoes, carrots and whole onions. Bring to a boil; reduce heat and simmer for 30 minutes or until the meatballs are done and vegetables are tender. Garnish with parsley. **Yield:** 8-10 servings.

UNSTUFFED CABBAGE

Mrs. Bernard Snow, Lewiston, Michigan
(PICTURED AT LEFT)

Here is one of my favorite ways to cook and enjoy cabbage. It has all the good flavor of regular cabbage rolls, but it's a lot less bother to make. In fact, it's a one-pot meal!

TOMATO SAUCE:
        1 large onion, chopped
        1 medium head cabbage, coarsely chopped
          (about 8 cups)
        1 can (8 ounces) tomato sauce
        1 can (28 ounces) tomatoes with liquid, cut up
        1 cup water
      1/4 cup lemon juice
      1/3 cup raisins
MEATBALLS:
        1 pound lean ground beef
      1/2 cup uncooked long grain rice
        1 teaspoon Worcestershire sauce
      1/2 teaspoon salt
      1/4 teaspoon pepper

Combine all of the sauce ingredients in a large skillet

STOVE-TOP SUCCESSES. Pictured at left, clockwise from bottom: Unstuffed Cabbage, Meatball Stew and Beef and Barley Mulligan (recipes on this page).

or Dutch oven. Bring to a boil; reduce heat and simmer. Meanwhile, combine meatball ingredients; mix well. Shape into 36 balls, about 1-1/4 in. in diameter. Add to simmering sauce. Cover and simmer about 45 minutes or until the cabbage is tender. Uncover and cook about 15 minutes longer or until sauce thickens. **Yield:** 6-8 servings.

BEEF AND BARLEY MULLIGAN

Dawn Supina, Edmonton, Alberta
(PICTURED AT LEFT)

This hearty recipe was in a handmade recipe book I received from a relative as a bridal shower gift.

    1-1/2 pounds lean ground beef
        1 medium onion, chopped
        1 medium green pepper, chopped
        1 can (16 ounces) tomatoes with liquid, cut up
        1 can (10-3/4 ounces) condensed beef broth,
          undiluted
        1 cup water
      3/4 cup medium pearl barley
        1 tablespoon brown sugar
        1 tablespoon vinegar
        1 teaspoon salt
      1/4 teaspoon pepper
      1/4 teaspoon garlic powder

In a large skillet, cook ground beef with onion and green pepper until the meat is browned and the vegetables are tender; drain. Stir in remaining ingredients; bring to a boil. Reduce heat; cover and simmer for about 1 hour or until barley is tender, stirring occasionally. **Yield:** 6-8 servings.

GREEN PEPPER CASSEROLE

Ellen Lloyd, Greenfield, Wisconsin

I always prepare this family favorite when peppers and onions are in season.

        3 pounds ground beef
        5 small onions, chopped
        3 cans (10-3/4 ounces *each*) condensed
          tomato soup, undiluted
        1 tablespoon paprika
        1 can (16 ounces) peas, drained
        3 medium green peppers, chopped
        1 can (8 ounces) sliced mushrooms, drained
        1 jar (4 ounces) diced pimiento, drained
Salt and pepper to taste
        1 box (16 ounces) shell macaroni
Grated Parmesan cheese

In a large skillet, brown beef with onions; drain. Add soup and paprika. Cover and simmer about 1 hour. Stir in peas, green pepper, mushrooms and pimiento. Simmer 15 minutes or until green pepper is tender. Season with salt and pepper. Meanwhile, cook macaroni according to package directions; rinse and drain. Place in a large serving bowl; cover with meat mixture. Sprinkle with Parmesan cheese. **Yield:** 12-16 servings.

GARDEN SKILLET SUPPER

Suzan Hatcher, Sand Springs, Oklahoma
(PICTURED AT RIGHT)

Our family gave this dish its name because I use whichever vegetables are in season in our garden patch. We grow and sell flowers, herbs, grapes, pumpkins and fruit plus eggs and honey—all on 3-1/2 acres of land!

  1 cup uncooked long grain rice
  1 tablespoon olive oil
  2 garlic cloves, minced
  1 cup chopped onion
1/2 cup chopped green pepper
1/2 cup chopped sweet red pepper
  1 pound ground beef, browned and drained
  2 cups chopped seeded tomatoes

Cook rice according to package directions. Meanwhile, heat oil in a skillet. Saute garlic, onion and peppers until tender. Stir in browned beef, tomatoes and rice; cook until heated through. **Yield:** 4-6 servings.

PIZZA POTATO TOPPERS

Sheila Friedrich, Antelope, Montana
(PICTURED AT RIGHT)

Not only is this recipe quick and easy to make, but it's an economical treat as well. I don't know of a more satisfying way to stretch a half pound of meat!

  4 medium baking potatoes
1/2 pound ground beef
1/2 cup chopped green pepper
  1 small onion chopped
  1 tomato, chopped
1/2 to 3/4 cup pizza sauce
  1 cup (4 ounces) shredded mozzarella cheese
Fresh oregano, basil *or* parsley, optional

Bake potatoes in a microwave or conventional oven. Meanwhile, in a skillet, cook beef with green pepper and onion until the meat is browned and the vegetables are tender; drain fat. Stir in tomato and pizza sauce; heat through. Split baked potatoes lengthwise; flake potato center with a fork. Spoon meat mixture into each; top with mozzarella cheese. Sprinkle with oregano, basil or parsley if desired. **Yield:** 4 servings.

HERBED ITALIAN MEAT SAUCE

LaVerne Creamer, Paducah, Texas
(PICTURED AT RIGHT)`

I got this recipe from a California cousin back in 1953, and it's just as popular with my family now as it was then. The slow simmering really blends the tastes.

  1 pound ground beef
1/2 cup chopped onion
  1 garlic clove, minced
  1 small green pepper, chopped
  1 can (28 ounces) stewed tomatoes
  2 cans (8 ounces *each*) tomato sauce
  1 can (8 ounces) sliced mushrooms, undrained

1-1/2 teaspoons salt
1/8 teaspoon pepper
  1 teaspoon ground sage
1/4 teaspoon dried thyme
  1 teaspoon dried rosemary
  1 bay leaf
  1 cup water
Cooked pasta
Grated Parmesan cheese

In a large skillet, cook ground beef and onion until the beef is browned and the onion is tender; drain. Stir in remaining ingredients except pasta and cheese. Simmer, uncovered, for 1-1/2 hours or until the sauce is as thick as desired, stirring occasionally. Serve over pasta; sprinkle with Parmesan cheese. **Yield:** 4-6 servings.

GERMAN SKILLET MEAL

Helen Phillips, Greensburg, Indiana

This was a quick, favorite meal when my children were growing up. I've entered my recipes in several contests and have won first- and second-place prizes.

  1 pound ground beef
  1 cup chopped onion
  1 cup uncooked long grain rice
  2 cans (8 ounces *each*) tomato sauce
  1 can (16 ounces) sauerkraut, undrained
1/2 teaspoon caraway seed
  1 cup water
1/2 teaspoon pepper
3/4 teaspoon salt, optional

In a skillet, cook ground beef and onion until the beef is browned and the onion is tender; drain. Stir in rice, tomato sauce, sauerkraut, caraway seed, water, pepper, and salt if desired. Bring to a boil. Reduce heat; cover and simmer about 25 minutes or until the rice is tender. **Yield:** 6 servings.

MACARONI WITH BEEF AND BEANS

Debbie Hagen, Mayville, North Dakota

My family enjoys this dish as an alternative to plain macaroni and cheese. Every summer and fall, I freeze lots of beans, as well as corn, carrots, green peppers and pumpkin, and I also make many varieties of pickles.

  1 pound ground beef
1/3 cup chopped onion
  1 can (16 ounces) tomatoes with liquid, cut up
  1 can (15 ounces) kidney beans, undrained
  2 to 3 teaspoons chili powder
  1 teaspoon salt
3/4 cup uncooked elbow macaroni

In a large skillet, brown beef and onion; drain fat. Add remaining ingredients. Cover and simmer for about 20 minutes, stirring occasionally, or until macaroni is tender. Thin with water if necessary. **Yield:** 4-6 servings.

> **EASY DOES IT!** Pictured at right, clockwise from bottom: Pizza Potato Toppers, Herbed Italian Meat Sauce and Garden Skillet Supper (all recipes on this page).

HONEY-GARLIC MEATBALLS

Barbara de Boer, Teeswater, Ontario

If you've never tried these two flavors together, you're in for a real treat! The garlic flavor is mellowed quite a bit by both the honey and the cooking process, so don't hesitate to use the full amount called for in this recipe.

        2 pounds ground beef
        1 cup dry bread crumbs
        2 eggs
        1 teaspoon salt
        1 tablespoon butter *or* margarine
        6 garlic cloves, minced
        3/4 cup ketchup
        1/2 cup honey
        1/4 cup soy sauce
    Cooked rice

Combine ground beef, bread crumbs, eggs and salt; mix well. Shape into 48 balls, about 1-1/2-in. in diameter. Place in a single layer on a jelly roll pan. Bake at 500° for 12-15 minutes, turning often; drain. Melt the butter in a large skillet; saute garlic until tender. Combine ketchup, honey and soy sauce; add to skillet. Bring to a boil. Reduce heat and simmer, covered, about 5 minutes. Add meatballs. Simmer, uncovered, until the sauce thickens and the meatballs are lightly glazed. Serve over rice. **Yield: 10-12 servings.**

HAYSTACKS WITH CHEESE SAUCE

Dorothy Krauss, Halstead, Kansas

Here's a recipe from my daughter that has a lot going for it. It's simple to toss together with ingredients I usually have on hand...and it's fun at the table, too, because everyone gets to build their own "haystack"!

    1-1/2 pounds ground beef
        2 tablespoons chopped onion
        1 can (10-3/4 ounces) condensed tomato
          soup, undiluted
        1 teaspoon chili powder
        1 teaspoon dried oregano
    1-1/2 teaspoons ground cumin
        1/4 teaspoon garlic powder
        1 teaspoon salt
        1/2 teaspoon pepper
    CHEESE SAUCE:
        4 tablespoons butter *or* margarine
        4 tablespoons all-purpose flour
        1 cup milk
        1 can (11 ounces) condensed cheddar cheese
          soup, undiluted
        1/2 pound process cheese, cubed
    Corn chips
    Cooked rice
    Shredded lettuce
    Picante sauce, optional

In a skillet, cook beef with onion until the beef is browned and the onion is tender; drain. Stir in tomato soup, chili powder, oregano, cumin, garlic powder, salt and pepper; simmer until heated through. For cheese sauce, melt butter in a saucepan. Add flour; cook and stir until a smooth paste forms. Gradually add milk; cook and stir until thickened. Stir in cheese soup. Add cheese; cook only until it melts. To serve, prepare individual corn chip "nests"; layer each with meat mixture, rice and lettuce. Top with cheese sauce, and picante sauce if desired. **Yield: 6-8 servings.**

HAMBURGER STEW

Margery Bryan, Royal City, Washington

There's nothing fancy to this recipe—it's just bursting with old-fashioned goodness and hearty flavor.

        1 pound ground beef
        1 envelope (1 ounce) dry onion soup mix
        1 can (16 ounces) tomatoes with liquid, cut up
        1 cup diced carrot
        1 cup diced peeled potato
        1 cup chopped cabbage
        2 cups frozen corn
        1 can (16 ounces) cut green beans *or* lima
          beans, drained
        1 tablespoon uncooked long grain rice
        2 to 3 cups water *or* tomato *or* vegetable juice

In a large skillet, cook ground beef; drain. Stir in the onion soup mix and tomatoes; simmer 10 minutes. Add carrot, potato, cabbage, corn and beans. Cover and simmer 20 minutes. Add rice and water or juice; bring to a boil. Reduce heat and simmer, covered, for 20 minutes or until the rice is cooked and the vegetables are tender. **Yield: 6-8 servings.**

BLACK-EYED PEAS SKILLET DINNER

Judy Wiles, Burlington, North Carolina

This recipe is a "lifesaver" when you need a meal in a hurry, which I discovered when our two boys were young and I was working outside the home. It also reheats well.

        1 pound ground beef
        1 medium onion, chopped
        1 medium green pepper, chopped
        2 cans (16 ounces *each*) black-eyed peas,
          drained
        1 can (16 ounces) tomatoes with liquid,
          chopped
        1/2 teaspoon salt
        1/2 teaspoon pepper

In a skillet, cook beef, onion and green pepper over medium heat until beef is browned; drain fat. Add peas, tomatoes, salt and pepper; bring to a boil. Reduce heat and simmer for 30 minutes, stirring often. **Yield: 4-6 servings.**

EGGPLANT SKILLET DINNER

Virginia Jung, Janesville, Wisconsin

My children always enjoyed this tasty dish. It was a great way to introduce them to eggplant.

        1 pound ground beef
        1/4 cup chopped onion

1 tablespoon all-purpose flour
1 can (8 ounces) tomato sauce
3/4 cup water
1/4 cup chopped green pepper
1 teaspoon dried oregano
1/2 to 1 teaspoon chili powder
1 small eggplant, cut into 1/2-inch slices
1/2 teaspoon salt
1/8 teaspoon pepper
1 cup (4 ounces) shredded process cheese
Grated Parmesan cheese, optional

In a skillet, brown beef with onion; drain. Sprinkle flour over beef; stir to mix. Add next five ingredients; mix well. Season eggplant with salt and pepper; arrange slices over meat mixture. Cover and simmer for 10-15 minutes or until eggplant is tender. Sprinkle with shredded cheese; cook until cheese melts. Serve with Parmesan cheese if desired. **Yield:** 4 servings.

— ■ ■ ■ —

SOUTHWEST ZUCCHINI SKILLET

Cathy Barkley, De Beque, Colorado

I like to serve this with corn bread. I also make sure to have extra salsa on hand for my husband—he likes his food spicy!

1 pound ground beef
1/2 teaspoon salt
1/2 cup chopped onion
4-1/2 cups chopped zucchini
1 can (16 ounces) tomatoes, drained and cut up
1 cup salsa
1 can (17 ounces) whole kernel corn, drained
1 can (16 ounces) chili beans
1 cup (8 ounces) sour cream
1-1/2 cups (6 ounces) shredded cheddar cheese

In a large skillet, brown beef with salt and onion; drain. Add zucchini, tomatoes and salsa. Cover and simmer about 20 minutes or until zucchini is crisp-tender. Add the corn and beans; cook until heated through. Remove from the heat. Gradually stir in sour cream; sprinkle with cheese. Cover and let stand until cheese melts. **Yield:** 6-8 servings.

— ■ ■ ■ —

SPAGHETTI CON CARNE

Carol Ice, Burlingham, New York

This is a hearty recipe that belonged to my grandparents, who homesteaded in Wyoming.

SAUCE:
1 teaspoon vegetable oil
1 garlic clove, minced
1 small onion, chopped
3 cups tomato juice
1 to 2 tablespoons chili powder
1 teaspoon salt
MEATBALLS:
1 pound ground beef
1 egg, beaten
1 garlic clove, minced
1 small onion, minced

1/4 cup yellow cornmeal
1 teaspoon salt
1/2 teaspoon pepper
1/2 teaspoon dried oregano
1 tablespoon vegetable oil
Cooked spaghetti

For sauce, heat oil in a large saucepan. Saute garlic and onion; add tomato juice, chili powder and salt. Simmer 10 minutes. In a bowl, mix first eight meatball ingredients. Shape into 3/4-in. meatballs. Heat oil in a skillet and brown meatballs on all sides. Add meatballs to sauce. Cover and simmer for 10 minutes or until the meatballs are cooked through. Serve over spaghetti. **Yield:** 4-6 servings.

— ■ ■ ■ —

SIX-LAYER DINNER

Charlotte McDaniel, Williamsville, Illinois

I originally came across a five-layer version of this dish at a Home Extension program. I increased the ground beef and added the celery myself, and my family prefers this version.

1-1/2 pounds ground beef
2 medium onions, sliced thin
3 medium potatoes, peeled and sliced thin
1 large green pepper, chopped
1-1/2 teaspoons salt
1/2 teaspoon pepper
2 celery stalks, chopped
1 can (16 ounces) stewed tomatoes
1/4 teaspoon dried basil

In a large Dutch oven, brown ground beef; drain fat. Cover beef with the onions, then potatoes and then green pepper, seasoning each layer lightly with salt and pepper. Put celery on top. Add tomatoes; sprinkle with basil. Bring to a boil. Reduce heat and simmer, covered, about 1 hour or until the vegetables are tender. **Yield:** 6-8 servings.

— ■ ■ ■ —

16TH-STREET STEW

Joseph Wouk, Williamsville, New York

Now that I've retired, I'm taking great delight in trying to emulate my wife, who is a great cook! This was my mother's recipe—she always called it "16th-Street Stew", but I never knew why.

1-1/2 pounds ground beef
1 medium onion, chopped
4 bacon strips, diced
1 green pepper, chopped
3 potatoes, peeled and diced
2 teaspoons prepared mustard
3 beef bouillon cubes
1/4 teaspoon pepper
2 cups boiling water
6 tablespoons vinegar

In a skillet, brown ground beef with onion, bacon and green pepper; drain. Add potatoes, mustard, bouillon and pepper. Stir in water and vinegar. Simmer over medium-low heat for 45 minutes or until the potatoes are tender. **Yield:** 4-6 servings.

Mexican Meals

TAMALE PIE
Ruth Aden, Polson, Montana
(PICTURED AT LEFT)

The amount of spice in this recipe is just right for my family, who prefers things on the mild side. Make it once with these measurements—then spice it up a little more if you like!

> 1-1/2 pounds ground beef
> 2 cans (14-1/2 ounces *each*) stewed tomatoes
> 1 medium onion, chopped
> 1/2 teaspoon garlic powder
> 1/2 teaspoon chili powder
> 1/4 teaspoon salt
> 1/4 teaspoon pepper
> 10 flour tortillas (6 inches)
> 3 cups (12 ounces) shredded Monterey Jack *or* Co-Jack cheese
> 1 can (2-1/4 ounces) sliced ripe olives, drained

In a skillet, brown ground beef; drain. Add tomatoes, onion and spices. Simmer, uncovered, for 20 minutes. Arrange five tortillas in the bottom of a 13-in. x 9-in. x 2-in. baking dish, tearing tortillas as needed. Cover with half of the meat mixture, then half of the cheese. Repeat layers, using remaining tortillas, meat mixture and cheese. Sprinkle with olives. Bake at 350° for 30 minutes or until heated through. Let stand a few minutes before serving. **Yield:** 8 servings.

MEATBALL CHILI WITH DUMPLINGS
Sarah Yoder, Middlebury, Indiana
(PICTURED AT LEFT)

My family enjoys this delicious recipe—it's like a spicy meatball stew with dumplings!

> 1 pound ground beef
> 3/4 cup finely chopped onion, *divided*
> 1/4 cup dry bread crumbs *or* rolled oats
> 1 egg
> 5 teaspoons instant beef bouillon granules, *divided*
> 3 teaspoons chili powder, *divided*
> 3 tablespoons all-purpose flour
> 1 tablespoon cooking oil
> 1 can (28 ounces) tomatoes with liquid, cut up
> 1 garlic clove, minced
> 1/2 teaspoon ground cumin
> 1 can (15-1/2 ounces) kidney beans, drained

CORNMEAL DUMPLINGS:
> 1-1/2 cups biscuit mix
> 1/2 cup yellow cornmeal
> 2/3 cup milk

In a large bowl, combine beef, 1/4 cup onion, bread crumbs or oats, egg, 3 teaspoons bouillon and 1 teaspoon chili powder. Shape into 12 meatballs, each 1-1/2 in. Roll in flour. Heat oil in a skillet; brown meatballs. Drain on paper towels. Meanwhile, in a large saucepan, combine tomatoes, garlic, cumin and remaining onion, bouillon and chili powder. Add meatballs. Cook, covered, on low heat for about 1 hour. Add the beans. For dumplings, combine all ingredients. Drop by spoonfuls into chili; cook on low, uncovered, for 10 minutes. Cover and cook 10-12 minutes longer. **Yield:** 6 servings.

TERRIFIC TACO SALAD
Jeannie Daubar, Todd, North Carolina
(PICTURED AT LEFT)

I invented this recipe several years ago. It's quick to make, and uses ingredients I usually have on hand in my pantry and refrigerator.

> 1 pound ground beef
> 1/2 teaspoon salt
> 1/4 teaspoon pepper
> 1 can (16 ounces) hot chili beans with gravy
> 4 to 6 cups corn chips
> 1 cup (4 ounces) shredded cheddar cheese
> 2 cups shredded lettuce
> 1 large tomato, chopped
> 1 small green pepper, chopped
> 6 green onions with tops, chopped
> 1 small avocado, chopped, optional
> 1/2 cup sliced ripe olives, optional
> 1 cup (8 ounces) sour cream
> Salsa

Brown ground beef; drain off fat. Season with salt and pepper; set aside. Heat beans in a saucepan. Divide meat mixture and beans into six portions. Assemble in layers on six plates the following: first layer—corn chips; second layer—beef mixture; third layer—cheese; fourth layer—chili beans; fifth layer—lettuce; and sixth layer—tomato, green pepper, onions, avocado and, if desired, olives. Top with a dollop of sour cream; pour salsa over all. **Yield:** 6 servings.

FIESTA FARE. Pictured at left, clockwise from top: Tamale Pie, Meatball Chili with Dumplings and Terrific Taco Salad (all recipes on this page).

■ ■ ■

ACAPULCO DELIGHT

Margene Skaggs, Guinda, California

This dish always delights family and friends at potlucks and gatherings I take it to.

   2 pounds ground beef
   1 envelope (1-1/4 ounces) taco seasoning
3/4 cup water
   2 jars (7 ounces *each*) green taco sauce
   9 flour tortillas (6 inches)
   2 cups (8 ounces) shredded cheddar cheese
   1 can (16 ounces) refried beans
   2 cups (16 ounces) sour cream
1/2 cup chopped green onions
   1 can (2-1/4 ounces) sliced ripe olives,
      drained

In a large skillet, brown beef; drain fat. Stir in taco seasoning and water. Add taco sauce; simmer for 5-10 minutes or until slightly thickened. Cover the bottom of a 13-in. x 9-in. x 2-in. baking dish with three tortillas, tearing them into pieces as necessary. Spread half of meat mixture over tortillas, then sprinkle with 1/2 cup cheese. Layer with three more tortillas; spread with refried beans. Cover with sour cream; sprinkle with green onions and olives. Place remaining tortillas over top; cover with remaining meat mixture and cheese. Bake at 350° for 25-30 minutes or until heated through. Let stand a few minutes before serving. **Yield:** 10 servings.

■ ■ ■

CORNMEAL EMPANADAS

Tammy Forbes, Lancaster, New Hampshire

My family enjoys having these beef turnovers in place of sandwiches for a change of pace. They freeze well and can be reheated in the microwave for a quick, hot meal.

FILLING:
1-1/2 pounds ground beef
1-1/2 cups thick spaghetti sauce
1/4 cup raisins
   2 teaspoons chili powder
   1 teaspoon brown sugar
1/2 teaspoon onion powder
1/2 teaspoon salt
1/4 teaspoon garlic powder
1/4 teaspoon ground cinnamon
CORNMEAL PASTRY:
   3 cups all-purpose flour
2/3 cup cornmeal
   1 teaspoon salt
   1 cup shortening
1/2 cup ice water
   1 egg, beaten
   1 tablespoon water
Taco sauce, optional

In a large skillet, brown beef; drain. Stir in spaghetti sauce, raisins and seasonings; simmer. Meanwhile, for pastry, combine flour, cornmeal and salt in a large bowl. Cut in shortening until mixture resembles coarse crumbs. Add ice water, a little at a time, until

dough forms a ball. Cover and let rest for 10 minutes. Divide pastry into two balls; roll half out on a lightly floured surface to a 16-in. circle. Cut into four 7-1/2-in. rounds. Place 1/2 cup filling on each round. Combine egg and water; brush on pastry edges. Fold dough over to form half circles; crimp edges to seal. Repeat with other half of pastry and remaining filling. Place on greased baking sheets; brush tops with remaining egg mixture. Bake at 400° for 25-30 minutes or until lightly browned. Serve with taco sauce if desired. **Yield:** 8 servings.

■ ■ ■

ENCHILADA CASSEROLE

Mildred Willett, Tillamook, Oregon

This recipe comes from my daughter, who is a wonderful cook. And that's my objective opinion!

   1 pound ground beef
   1 large onion, chopped
1/4 cup chopped green pepper
   1 can (14-1/2 ounces) whole tomatoes,
      chopped and drained
   1 can (10 ounces) enchilada sauce
   1 can (2-1/4 ounces) sliced ripe olives, drained
   1 teaspoon salt
   2 cups (8 ounces) shredded cheddar cheese,
      divided
   1 cup cottage cheese
   1 egg, beaten
   1 package (10 ounces) corn tortillas
      (6 inches), torn into pieces

In a skillet, cook ground beef with onion and green pepper until the beef is browned and vegetables are tender; drain. Stir in tomatoes, enchilada sauce, olives and salt. Cover and simmer about 20 minutes. Meanwhile, combine 1 cup cheddar cheese, cottage cheese and egg; mix well. Set aside. Spread one-third of the meat mixture into a greased 13-in. x 9-in. x 2-in. baking dish. Cover with half of the tortillas; spread with half of the cheese mixture. Repeat layers with remaining ingredients, ending with the meat mixture. Bake at 350° for 30 minutes. Remove from oven and sprinkle with remaining cheddar cheese. Return to oven for 3-5 minutes or until cheese is melted. Let stand 5-10 minutes before serving. **Yield:** 6-8 servings.

■ ■ ■

BEEFY ENCHILADAS

Connie Shay, Kennewick, Washington

This family favorite is a meal-in-one with salad or fruit. Tortilla chips are also good served with it.

1-1/2 pounds ground beef
1/2 cup chopped onion
   1 can (16 ounces) refried beans
1/2 teaspoon salt
1/4 teaspoon pepper
   2 tomatoes, chopped
  10 corn tortillas (6 inches)

SAUCE:
- 4 tablespoons butter *or* margarine
- 1/4 cup all-purpose flour
- 2 cups milk
- 1 can (10 ounces) enchilada sauce
- 1-1/2 cups (6 ounces) shredded cheddar cheese
- 3/4 cup sliced ripe olives

In a skillet, brown beef and onion until beef is no longer pink and onion is tender. Drain fat. Stir in beans, salt and pepper. Place 1/3 cup of mixture and a spoonful of tomatoes on each tortilla. Roll up and place, seam side down, in a 13-in. x 9-in. x 2-in. baking pan. For sauce, melt butter in a saucepan. Stir in flour until smooth. Add milk and enchilada sauce; stir until smooth. Add cheese and olives; cook over medium-high until mixture boils. Pour over enchiladas. Bake at 350° for 30 minutes. **Yield:** 5-6 servings.

Mexican Lasagna
Brenda Cooper, Edna, Kansas

Our friends and family love this recipe. It's easy to make ahead of time and can be frozen. This is especially nice during particularly busy times of the year.

- 2 pounds ground beef
- 1/2 cup chopped onion
- 1 jar (24 ounces) picante sauce
- 1 can (15 ounces) chili beans *or* pinto beans with jalapenos, undrained
- 1 teaspoon salt
- 1/2 teaspoon pepper
- 2 cups cottage cheese
- 1 egg, beaten
- 2 cups (8 ounces) shredded Monterey Jack cheese
- 12 corn tortillas (6 inches)
- 1 cup (4 ounces) shredded cheddar cheese
- 1/2 cup thinly sliced green onions, optional
- 1/2 cup sour cream, optional

In a large skillet, cook beef and onion until the beef is browned and onion is tender. Drain fat. Stir in picante sauce, beans, salt and pepper; set aside. In a small bowl, combine cottage cheese and egg. Spread one-third of meat mixture in the bottom of one 13-in. x 9-in. x 2-in. baking pan or two 8-in. square baking pans. Top with half of Monterey Jack cheese, half of cottage cheese mixture and six tortillas (tear tortillas if necessary to cover cheese more completely). Repeat layers, ending with meat. Sprinkle with cheddar cheese. Bake at 350° for 45-50 minutes. Let stand a few minutes before serving. Garnish with green onions and serve with sour cream if desired. **Yield:** 10 servings.

Taco Casserole
Juanita Gilliam, Tillamook, Oregon

This casserole makes a very filling main dish and the chicken soup adds a tasty flavor, too!

- 1 pound ground beef

- 1 medium onion, chopped
- 1 package (1-1/4 ounces) taco seasoning
- 1 can (8 ounces) tomato sauce
- 1 can (10-3/4 ounces) condensed cream of chicken soup, undiluted
- 1 cup (8 ounces) sour cream
- 1 can (4 ounces) chopped green chilies, drained
- 2 flour tortillas (10 inches)
- 2 cups (8 ounces) shredded cheddar cheese

In a skillet, brown beef and onion; drain fat. Stir in taco seasoning and tomato sauce; set aside. In a large bowl, mix together soup, sour cream and chilies. Place one tortilla in the bottom of a 10-in. pie plate. Combine beef mixture with half of soup mixture; spoon over tortilla. Sprinkle with 1 cup cheese; top with second tortilla. Top with remaining soup mixture and sprinkle with remaining cheese. Bake at 350° for about 30 minutes or until heated through. Let stand a few minutes before serving. **Yield:** 8 servings.

Cheesy Tortilla Bake
Diane Hansen, Prairie Farm, Wisconsin

The from-scratch tortillas in this dish couldn't be simpler or easier to make. These enchiladas freeze well, too.

TORTILLAS:
- 1 cup all-purpose flour
- 1/2 cup yellow cornmeal
- 1/2 teaspoon salt
- 1-2/3 cups milk
- 1 egg, beaten
- 2 teaspoons butter *or* margarine, melted

FILLING:
- 1 pound ground beef
- 1/2 cup chopped onion
- 1 garlic clove, minced
- 1 can (10-3/4 ounces) condensed tomato soup, undiluted
- 1 can (10-3/4 ounces) condensed cream of mushroom soup, undiluted
- 1/2 cup taco sauce
- 1 teaspoon dried oregano
- 1 can (2-1/4 ounces) sliced ripe olives, drained
- 2 cups (8 ounces) shredded cheddar cheese

Combine flour, cornmeal and salt in a mixing bowl. Add milk, egg and butter. Beat until smooth. Place a lightly greased small skillet over medium heat. For each tortilla, pour about 3 tablespoons of batter into skillet. Lift and tilt skillet to spread batter. Return to heat. Cook until light brown; turn and brown the other side. Remove to a warm platter; repeat with remaining batter. Set aside. For filling, cook ground beef, onion and garlic until the meat is browned and onion is tender; drain. Stir in soups, taco sauce, oregano and olives. Meanwhile, cover the bottom of a 12-in. x 8-in. x 2-in. baking dish with six tortillas, overlapping as needed. Cover with half of meat mixture. Top with remaining tortillas and remaining meat mixture. Sprinkle with cheese. Bake at 350° for 30 minutes or until heated through. Let stand a few minutes before serving. **Yield:** 8 servings.

FOLD-OVER TORTILLA BAKE

Deborah Smith, DeWitt, Nebraska
(PICTURED AT LEFT)

Here's something a little different from the usual tacos—and it's special enough for potlucks or dinner guests.

    1 pound ground beef
    1 cup chopped onion
    2 cans (14-1/2 ounces *each*) stewed tomatoes
    1 cup enchilada sauce
    1 to 2 teaspoons ground cumin
 1/2 teaspoon salt
 1/4 teaspoon pepper
   12 flour *or* corn tortillas (6 inches)
    2 packages (3 ounces *each*) cream cheese, softened
    1 can (4 ounces) chopped green chilies, drained
    1 cup (4 ounces) shredded Monterey Jack cheese

In a skillet, cook ground beef and onion until the beef is browned and onion is tender; drain well. Stir in tomatoes, enchilada sauce and seasonings. Bring to a boil. Reduce heat and simmer, covered, for 5 minutes. Pour half of the meat sauce into a 13-in. x 9-in. x 2-in. baking dish. Set aside. Wrap the stack of tortillas in foil; warm at 350° for 8-10 minutes. Spread warm tortillas with cream cheese and top with chilies. Fold tortillas in half. Arrange folded tortillas over meat sauce; pour remaining sauce over top. Cover and bake at 350° for 15 minutes. Sprinkle with cheese and bake another 5 minutes or until cheese is melted. **Yield:** 6 servings.

PRONTO PINWHEELS

Eileen Owen, Johnstown, Colorado
(PICTURED AT LEFT)

Serve this pretty dish with a crisp lettuce salad and top it off with fresh fruit or a lemony dessert, and you have a complete meal your family will love!

1-1/2 pounds lean ground beef
 1/4 cup finely chopped onion
    5 ounces condensed vegetable beef soup, undiluted
 1/2 teaspoon chili powder
    1 can (4 ounces) chopped green chilies, drained
 1/2 cup quick-cooking oats
    2 tubes (7-1/2 ounces *each*) refrigerated biscuits
   16 thin tomato slices
 1/2 cup sliced ripe olives
    1 medium green pepper, chopped
1-1/2 cups (6 ounces) shredded cheddar cheese

In a large bowl, combine first six ingredients. Mix well and set aside. Roll biscuits into an 18-in. x 9-in. rectangle and top with meat mixture. Roll rectangle, jelly-roll style, starting from wide end. Seal seams. Cut into 1-in. slices. Place slices in two greased 9-in. pie plates. Cover with foil and bake at 350° for 15 minutes. Uncover and bake 10 minutes longer. Remove from oven; top each pinwheel with a tomato slice, olives, green pepper and cheese. Return to oven for a few minutes or until cheese is melted. **Yield:** 16 servings.

TACOS DELUXE

Katie Dreibelbis, Santa Clara, California
(PICTURED AT LEFT)

I first tried this recipe in my junior high school home economics class some 20 years ago. As an adult, I wrote home for the recipe and have enjoyed it ever since!

    1 pound ground beef
    2 tablespoons chopped onion
    1 can (15 ounces) tomato sauce
    1 teaspoon vinegar
    1 teaspoon Worcestershire sauce
    2 to 3 drops hot pepper sauce
    1 teaspoon sugar
    1 teaspoon chili powder
 1/2 teaspoon garlic salt
 1/4 teaspoon celery salt
 1/4 teaspoon onion salt
 1/8 teaspoon ground allspice
 1/8 teaspoon ground cinnamon
Dash pepper
 1/2 cup shredded cheddar cheese
    6 to 8 taco shells
Shredded lettuce
Chopped tomatoes
SWEET-AND-SOUR DRESSING:
    1 cup salad dressing
 1/3 cup sugar
    2 tablespoons vinegar
 1/4 teaspoon salt
 1/2 teaspoon hot pepper sauce

In a skillet, brown ground beef and onion; drain. Add the next 12 ingredients to meat mixture. Simmer, uncovered, for 10 to 15 minutes or until most of the moisture evaporates, stirring occasionally. Cool slightly; stir in cheese. Put taco shells open end up in a baking pan; place scoopful of meat mixture into each shell. Bake at 400° for 10-15 minutes until meat is hot and cheese is melted. Sprinkle lettuce and tomatoes over tacos. Combine all dressing ingredients and drizzle over tacos. **Yield:** 6-8 servings.

SPICY SPECIALTIES. Pictured at left from top to bottom: Fold-Over Tortilla Bake, Pronto Pinwheels and Tacos Deluxe (all recipes on this page).

TEXAS ENCHILADAS
Norma Davis, Ouray, Colorado

Whenever I'm feeling homesick for my native state of Texas, I make this authentic recipe. But you sure don't have to be a Texan to enjoy it!

    1 pound ground beef
    1 small onion, chopped
    1 teaspoon chili powder
Salt and pepper to taste
    3 cups (12 ounces) shredded cheddar cheese,
      divided
   12 corn tortillas (10 inches)
SAUCE:
    2 tablespoons butter *or* margarine
    2 tablespoons all-purpose flour
    1 can (15 ounces) tomato sauce
    1 tablespoon chili powder
  1/4 teaspoon salt
Dash cayenne pepper

In a skillet, cook ground beef and onion until the meat is browned and onion is tender; drain. Stir in chili powder, salt, pepper and 1-1/2 cups cheese. Soften tortillas according to package directions. Spoon about 1/4 cup of meat mixture onto each tortilla. Roll up and place, seam side down, in a greased 13-in. x 9-in. x 2-in. baking dish; set aside. For sauce, melt butter in a small saucepan. Stir in flour; cook until bubbly. Add remaining sauce ingredients. Cook, stirring constantly, until the mixture thickens. Pour over tortillas. Sprinkle with remaining cheese. Bake at 350° for 30 minutes or until heated through and bubbly. **Yield:** 6-8 servings.

SOUTH-OF-THE-BORDER STEW
Dlores DeWitt, Colorado Springs, Colorado

A friend gave me this recipe many years ago and my family just loves it! Feel free to increase the amount of seasonings to suit your own taste.

    1 pound ground beef
  3/4 cup chopped onion
  1/2 teaspoon dried oregano
  1/2 teaspoon hot pepper sauce
    1 garlic clove, minced
    1 can (4 ounces) chopped green chilies
    1 can (8 ounces) tomato sauce
    1 can (16 ounces) stewed tomatoes
    2 cans (15 ounces *each*) chili beans with gravy

In a skillet, brown ground beef and onion; drain. Add spices and remaining ingredients. Cover and simmer 1 hour. **Yield:** 6 servings.

TEX-MEX CASSEROLE
Cheryl Ruesch, Waukegan, Illinois

Both family and friends enjoy this dish—even those who prefer a level of spiciness that's "mild" rather than "wild" (but still full of flavor!).

    2 pounds ground beef

    1 onion, chopped
    1 teaspoon garlic powder
    1 can (10-3/4 ounces) condensed cream of
      mushroom soup, undiluted
    1 can (10-3/4 ounces) condensed cream of
      chicken soup, undiluted
    2 cans (8 ounces *each*) mild enchilada sauce
  3/4 cup milk
  30 crisp taco shells, broken
    2 cups (8 ounces) shredded cheddar cheese

In a skillet, cook ground beef with onion and garlic powder until meat is browned and onion is tender; drain. Stir in soups, enchilada sauce and milk. Place half of the broken taco shells in a 13-in. x 9-in. x 2-in. baking dish. Layer with half of the meat mixture and half of the cheese. Repeat layers using remaining taco shells, meat mixture and cheese. Bake at 350° for about 45 minutes or until heated through. Let stand a few minutes before serving. **Yield:** 10-12 servings.

MEXICAN CORN BREAD
Elizabeth Sanders, Obion, Tennessee

Our family enjoys this beef-stuffed corn bread with a simple side dish like stewed tomatoes, beans, slaw or greens.

    2 eggs
  2/3 cup vegetable oil
    1 cup (8 ounces) sour cream
1-1/2 cups self-rising cornmeal
    2 tablespoons chopped green pepper
    2 tablespoons chopped onion
    2 tablespoons chopped pimiento
    1 can (4 ounces) chopped green chilies,
      drained
    1 pound ground beef, cooked and drained
1-1/2 cups (6 ounces) shredded cheddar cheese

In a mixing bowl, combine eggs, oil and sour cream. Stir in cornmeal, green pepper, onion, pimiento and chilies; mix well. Pour half of cornmeal mixture into a greased 12-in. x 8-in. x 2-in. baking dish. Top with beef. Sprinkle with 1/2 cup cheddar cheese. Spoon remaining cornmeal mixture over cheese. Sprinkle with remaining cheese. Bake at 350° for 30 minutes or until bread tests done. **Yield:** 10 servings.

SOUR CREAM CHILI BAKE
Nancy Baggett, Lawton, Oklahoma

The crushed corn chips add a crunchy contrast to the other ingredients in this casserole. It's an often-requested recipe at the Baggett home!

    1 pound ground beef
    1 can (16 ounces) pinto beans, drained
    1 can (15 ounces) hot chili beans with gravy
    1 can (10 ounces) enchilada sauce
    1 can (8 ounces) tomato sauce
    1 teaspoon chili powder
1-1/2 cups (6 ounces) shredded cheddar cheese,
      divided
    1 tablespoon dried minced onion

2 cups corn chips, crushed, *divided*
1 cup (8 ounces) sour cream

In a skillet, brown ground beef; drain. Stir in beans, enchilada sauce, tomato sauce, chili powder, 1 cup cheese, onion and 1 cup corn chips. Pour into a 2-qt. casserole dish. Cover and bake at 375° for 30 minutes. Remove from oven and spoon sour cream over casserole. Sprinkle with remaining 1/2 cup cheese and 1 cup corn chips. Return to oven and bake, uncovered, for 2-3 minutes or until cheese is melted. **Yield:** 8-10 servings.

■ ■ ■

Enchilada Lasagna
Diane McCann, Sterling, Colorado

I adapted this recipe from one I got from a television program. The refried beans were a last-minute inspiration when company was coming and I didn't have enough ground beef thawed out! They add extra goodness to this hearty, cheesy dish.

2 pounds ground beef
1 medium onion, chopped
2 garlic cloves, minced
1 can (10-3/4 ounces) condensed tomato soup, undiluted
1 cup picante sauce *or* salsa
1 can (16 ounces) refried beans
10 flour tortillas (6 inches)
4 cups (16 ounces) shredded cheddar cheese

In a skillet, cook ground beef, onion and garlic until the meat is browned and onion is tender; drain. Stir in tomato soup, picante sauce or salsa and refried beans. Heat thoroughly. Arrange five tortillas in a 12-in. x 8-in. x 2-in. baking dish, tearing tortillas as needed to cover the bottom. Layer with half of the meat mixture and half of the cheese. Repeat layers using remaining tortillas, meat mixture and cheese. Bake at 350° for 30 minutes or until heated through. Let stand a few minutes before serving. **Yield:** 10 servings.

■ ■ ■

Southwest Skillet Supreme
Connie Isaacson, Globe, Arizona

This is the kind of dish that's popular among cattle ranchers in Arizona. I've even won two cooking contests including a cattle growers "beef cook-off" with this recipe!

2 pounds ground beef
1-1/2 cups chopped onion
1 teaspoon dried oregano
1 teaspoon salt
1 teaspoon sugar
2 teaspoons chili powder
1 can (16 ounces) pinto beans with liquid
1 can (11 ounces) Mexican-style kernel corn, drained
3 cans (8 ounces *each*) tomato sauce
1-1/2 cups (6 ounces) shredded cheddar cheese
Tortilla chips
2 cups shredded lettuce
2 tomatoes, chopped

1 can (2-1/2 ounces) sliced ripe olives, drained
1/3 cup sour cream

In a skillet, cook ground beef with onion until the beef is browned and onion is tender; drain. Stir in next seven ingredients; simmer 15 minutes. Leave in skillet or spoon into a shallow serving dish; sprinkle with cheese and circle with tortilla chips. Garnish with lettuce, tomato, olives and sour cream. **Yield:** 8-10 servings.

■ ■ ■

Texican Rice Salad
Rebecca Mininger, El Campo, Texas

This dish is a favorite of my husband's and makes use of the plentiful rice grown in our area. I make it often!

1 pound ground beef
1/2 cup chopped onion
1/2 cup chili sauce
2 garlic cloves, minced
1/2 teaspoon salt
1 teaspoon chili powder
3 cups cooked rice
1 can (15 ounces) garbanzo beans, drained
1 can (4 ounces) chopped green chilies
1 to 2 medium tomatoes, seeded and chopped
Shredded lettuce
Shredded cheddar cheese

In a skillet, brown ground beef and onion; drain. In a small bowl, combine chili sauce, garlic, salt and chili powder; add to meat mixture. Add rice, beans and chilies; mix well. Cover and cook over medium until heated through. Add tomato; cook 5 minutes more. For each serving, spoon 1 cup meat mixture over lettuce and sprinkle with cheese. **Yield:** 8-10 servings.

■ ■ ■

Hamburger Chilaquiles
Karen Mefford, East Camden, Arkansas

The name is pronounced "chee-la-KEE-lays"...whenever I make it, friends and family pronounce it "delicious"!

1 pound ground beef
1 medium onion, chopped
1 package (1-1/4 ounces) taco seasoning
1 can (4 ounces) chopped green chilies
1 can (28 ounces) whole tomatoes with liquid, cut up
1/2 package (12 ounces) tortilla chips
4 cups (16 ounces) shredded Monterey Jack cheese
1/2 cup sour cream
1 cup (4 ounces) shredded cheddar cheese

In a skillet, cook ground beef and onion until meat is browned and onion is tender; drain. Stir in taco seasoning, chilies and tomatoes. Simmer, uncovered, for 15 minutes. Place half the tortilla chips in a 13-in. x 9-in. x 2-in. baking dish. Layer half of the meat mixture and half of the Monterey Jack cheese over the tortilla chips. Repeat layers. Bake at 350° for 20 minutes. Remove from oven. Top with dollops of sour cream. Sprinkle with cheddar cheese and bake another 10 minutes or until heated through. **Yield:** 8 servings.

SOUTH-OF-THE-BORDER SENSATIONS.
Clockwise from top right: Chili 'n' Cheese
Enchiladas (p. 92), Enchilada Torte (p. 92),
Giant Empanadas (p. 92), Navajo Tacos (p.
92) and Beef, Rice and Chili Casserole (p. 93).

CHILI 'N' CHEESE ENCHILADAS

Kim Prorok, North Fort Myers, Florida
(PICTURED ON PAGE 91)

I combined two of my family's favorite flavors to invent this dish—and ever since, I've gotten more requests for it than I can remember!

1 pound ground beef
1-1/2 cups chopped onion, *divided*
1 package (1-1/4 ounces) chili seasoning
1 can (8 ounces) tomato sauce
1 can (6 ounces) tomato paste
1 can (15 ounces) chili beans with gravy
1/2 cup water
2-1/2 cups (10 ounces) shredded cheddar cheese, *divided*
6 flour tortillas (6 inches)
1 jar (8 ounces) picante sauce

In a large ovenproof skillet, cook ground beef and 1/2 cup onion until the meat is browned and onion is tender. Drain. Stir in chili seasoning, tomato sauce, tomato paste, chili beans and water. Simmer, uncovered, for 15 minutes. Meanwhile, combine 2 cups cheese and remaining onion. Divide cheese mixture evenly on the tortillas. Roll up each tortilla and arrange, seam side down, on top of the chili mixture. Top with picante sauce and remaining cheese. Bake at 350° for 20-25 minutes or until heated through. **Yield:** 6 servings.

ENCHILADA TORTE

Anna Mae Ackerman, Spearville, Kansas
(PICTURED ON PAGE 91)

We are crazy about Mexican food at our house and are always trying new recipes. This stack of tortillas with all the different fillings really hits the spot!

1 pound ground beef
7 flour tortillas (10 inches)
1 jar (8 ounces) taco sauce
1 large onion, chopped
2 cups (8 ounces) shredded cheddar cheese
1 can (16 ounces) refried beans
1 can (2-1/2 ounces) sliced ripe olives, drained
1 can (4 ounces) chopped green chilies
1 cup (8 ounces) sour cream
1 large green pepper, chopped
2 cups (8 ounces) shredded Monterey Jack cheese
1 can (8 ounces) enchilada sauce
Shredded Monterey Jack and cheddar cheeses, optional

In a skillet, brown ground beef until no longer pink; drain fat. Meanwhile, place one tortilla in a 12-in. round casserole or on a large baking sheet or pizza pan. Layer half each of taco sauce, beef, onion and cheddar cheese on the tortilla. Top with second tortilla and press gently; layer half of the refried beans, olives and chilies. Top with third tortilla and layer half

each of sour cream, green pepper and Monterey Jack cheese. Top with fourth tortilla and top with remaining taco sauce, beef, onion and cheddar cheese. On the fifth tortilla, layer remaining beans, olives and chilies. On the sixth tortilla, layer remaining sour cream, green pepper and Monterey Jack cheese. Top with last tortilla; spread with enchilada sauce. Bake at 350° for 1 hour. Let stand a few minutes before cutting into wedges. Sprinkle with additional Monterey Jack and cheddar cheeses if desired. **Yield:** 10-12 servings.

GIANT EMPANADAS

Dianne Stonewall, Danville, Illinois
(PICTURED ON PAGE 91)

Serve these south-of-the-border meat pies whenever your family has worked up an especially hearty appetite. You'll see satisfied smiles all around the table just as I do!

1 pound ground beef
1 cup chopped onion
1 cup chopped green pepper
1 can (14-1/2 ounces) whole tomatoes with liquid, cut up
1 tablespoon chili powder
1 teaspoon ground cumin
1/2 teaspoon salt
1/2 teaspoon pepper
2 unbaked pie pastries (9 inches *each*)
1 egg yolk
1 tablespoon water
Sour cream, chopped fresh tomatoes *and/or* shredded cheese and lettuce for garnish, optional

In a skillet, brown beef with onion and green pepper. Drain. Stir in tomatoes and seasonings. Simmer, uncovered, for 15 minutes, stirring occasionally. Place pie pastries on a baking sheet. Divide filling; spoon half of filling on one half of each pastry, spreading to within 1 in. of edges. Fold other half of pastry over filling and press edges to seal. Beat egg yolk with water; brush over pastries. Bake at 400° for about 20 minutes or until golden. Cut into wedges to serve. Garnish with sour cream, tomatoes, cheese and/or lettuce if desired. **Yield:** 6 servings.

NAVAJO TACOS

Robin Wells, Tulsa, Oklahoma
(PICTURED ON PAGE 90)

My niece gave me this hearty recipe. It came from a Native American friend of hers in Eufaula, Oklahoma.

1 loaf frozen white bread dough, thawed
FILLING:
1 pound ground beef
1 pound hot bulk pork sausage
1 package (1-1/4 ounces) taco seasoning
1 can (15 ounces) pinto beans, drained and rinsed
1/2 cup water
Cooking oil
Chopped tomato

Finely chopped onion
Shredded lettuce
Shredded cheddar cheese
Taco sauce

Allow dough to rise. Meanwhile, for filling, brown ground beef and sausage in a skillet; drain. Stir in taco seasoning, beans and water. Simmer 15-20 minutes or until the water is almost evaporated; set aside. After dough rises, punch down. Make tortillas by dividing dough into 10 to 12 equal balls. Using a small amount of flour, roll each ball into an 8-in. circle (tortillas should be thin). Fry each tortilla in 1/4-in. of hot oil until golden, turning once. Drain tortillas on paper towels; keep warm. Top each tortilla with meat mixture, tomato, onion, lettuce, cheese and taco sauce. **Yield:** 10-12 servings.

■ ■ ■

BEEF, RICE AND CHILI CASSEROLE

June Howard, Athol, Idaho
(PICTURED ON PAGE 90)

There's nothing to assembling this hearty, satisfying dish. Men especially like it—they never leave the table hungry!

      1/2 pound ground beef
        1 cup chopped celery
      1/2 cup chopped onion
        1 small green pepper, chopped
        1 garlic clove, minced
        2 cups cooked rice
        1 can (15 ounces) chili con carne with beans
      2/3 cup mayonnaise
Few drops hot pepper sauce
      1/2 teaspoon salt
        1 can (14-1/2 ounces) Mexican-style stewed tomatoes
        1 to 2 cups (4 to 8 ounces) shredded cheddar cheese
        4 cups corn chips

In a skillet, cook ground beef, celery, onion, green pepper and garlic until meat is browned and vegetables are tender; drain. Stir in rice, chili, mayonnaise, hot pepper sauce, salt and tomatoes. Pour mixture into a 2-1/2-qt. casserole. Bake at 350° for 35-45 minutes or until heated through. Top with cheese and corn chips. Return to oven for 3 to 4 minutes or until cheese is melted. Let stand a few minutes before serving. **Yield:** 6-8 servings.

■ ■ ■

MEXICAN PIE

Denise Simeth, Greendale, Wisconsin

This recipe combines a ground beef main dish with a rice side dish to make a hearty, satisfying meal. I prepare this pie often because my husband loves it—and he always asks for second helpings!

RICE CRUST:
        2 cups beef broth
        1 cup uncooked long grain rice
        1 tablespoon butter *or* margarine

        1 teaspoon salt
        2 eggs, beaten
        2 tablespoons chopped pimiento
FILLING:
        1 pound ground beef
        1 garlic clove, minced
        1 teaspoon ground cumin
      1/2 cup bottled mild taco sauce
        1 egg, beaten
GUACAMOLE:
        1 large avocado
        1 tablespoon chopped onion
        1 tablespoon bottled mild taco sauce
      1/2 teaspoon lemon juice
        1 cup (8 ounces) sour cream

In a medium saucepan, combine beef broth, rice, butter and salt. Cover and cook rice according to package directions. Remove from heat; cool slightly. Stir in eggs and pimiento. Press into the bottom and up the sides of a greased 10-in. pie plate; set aside. For filling, brown ground beef in a skillet; drain. Stir in garlic and cumin; cook 2 minutes. Remove from heat; stir in taco sauce and egg. Spoon filling into crust. Bake at 350° for 25 minutes. Meanwhile, for guacamole, mash avocado with a fork in a small bowl. Stir in onion, taco sauce and lemon juice; cover and set aside. Remove pie from oven; spread guacamole over meat. Top with sour cream. Return to oven for 5 minutes. **Yield:** 6 servings.

■ ■ ■

CHILI RELLENO CASSEROLE

Joan Schroeder, Pinedale, Wyoming

The traditional recipe for chili relleno takes more time to prepare than this casserole version.

        1 pound ground beef
        1 green pepper, chopped
      1/2 teaspoon salt
      1/4 teaspoon pepper
      1/4 teaspoon dried oregano
      1/8 teaspoon garlic powder
        2 cups (8 ounces) shredded cheddar cheese
        2 cups (8 ounces) shredded Monterey Jack cheese
        2 cans (4 ounces *each*) chopped green chilies
        4 eggs, beaten
        1 cup light cream
        1 tablespoon all-purpose flour
        1 can (8 ounces) tomato sauce
Additional shredded cheddar cheese, optional

In a skillet, brown ground beef; drain. Add green pepper, salt, pepper, oregano and garlic powder. Cook until green pepper is tender. Combine cheddar and Monterey Jack cheeses; set aside. In a 2-1/2-qt. casserole dish, layer half each of meat mixture, chilies and cheese; repeat with remaining meat mixture, chilies and cheese. Meanwhile, in a mixing bowl, combine eggs, cream and flour; pour over cheese layer. Bake at 350° for 35 minutes. Remove from oven; cover with tomato sauce. Sprinkle with additional cheese if desired. Bake 10-15 minutes longer or until casserole is set. **Yield:** 6-8 servings.

Fiesta Surprise

Jan Seibert, Albion, California

(PICTURED AT LEFT)

I have a friend who is a native Californian, but developed this dish during 30 years of living in Alaska. She made it whenever she yearned for "food like back home".

        1-1/2 pounds ground beef
            1 medium onion, chopped
            1 package (1-1/4 ounces) taco seasoning
            1 cup water
        1/2 cup bottled red taco sauce
           10 corn tortillas (6 inches)
            2 packages (10 ounces *each*) frozen chopped
                 spinach, thawed and partially drained
            3 cups (12 ounces) shredded Monterey Jack
                 cheese
        1/2 cup chopped fully cooked ham
            1 cup (8 ounces) sour cream

In a skillet, cook ground beef and onion until the beef is browned and onion is tender; drain. Stir in taco seasoning and water. Cover and simmer for 10 minutes. Pour 1/4 cup taco sauce in a 12-in. x 8-in. x 2-in. baking pan; coat five tortillas on both sides with the sauce. Overlap the tortillas to make bottom layer. Mix one package of spinach into the beef mixture and spoon over the tortillas. Top with half of the cheese. Cover with remaining tortillas, overlapping as needed. Spread with remaining red taco sauce. Sprinkle with ham; cover with sour cream. Sprinkle remaining spinach over top; cover with remaining cheese. Bake at 350° for 45 minutes or until heated through. Let stand a few minutes before serving. **Yield:** 8-10 servings.

■ ■ ■

Mexican Pasta Bake

Joy Smith, Bigfork, Minnesota

(PICTURED AT LEFT)

This casserole makes a delicious change of pace from ordinary pasta casseroles. The corkscrew noodles? They make it fun!

            1 pound ground beef
            1 package (1-1/4 ounces) taco seasoning
            1 can (15 ounces) tomato sauce
        1/4 cup chopped green pepper
            1 teaspoon garlic powder
            1 teaspoon dried oregano
            8 ounces corkscrew noodles, cooked
            1 cup (4 ounces) shredded cheddar cheese
        1/2 cup sour cream

In a skillet, brown ground beef; drain. Stir in taco seasoning, tomato sauce, green pepper and spices. Bring

to a boil; remove from heat. Meanwhile, combine pasta, 1/2 cup cheese and sour cream. Spoon into the bottom of greased 2-qt. baking dish. Top with meat mixture and remaining cheese. Bake, uncovered, at 350° for 30 minutes. **Yield:** 6 servings.

■ ■ ■

Layered Tortilla Pie

Delma Snyder, McCook, Nebraska

(PICTURED AT LEFT)

This is a nice dish for potluck dinners and picnics—my family really devours it whenever I serve it! My sister used to serve tortilla pie at the hunting and fishing lodge she operated in Colorado.

            1 pound ground beef
            1 medium onion, chopped
            1 can (8 ounces) tomato sauce
            1 garlic clove, minced
            1 tablespoon chili powder
        1/2 teaspoon salt
        1/4 teaspoon pepper
            1 can (2-1/2 ounces) sliced ripe olives,
                 drained, optional
            1 tablespoon butter *or* margarine
            6 corn tortillas (6 inches)
            2 cups (8 ounces) shredded cheddar
                 cheese
        1/4 cup water

In a skillet, brown beef and onion; drain fat. Add tomato sauce, garlic, chili powder, salt and pepper. Add olives if desired. Mix well and simmer for 5 minutes. Lightly butter tortillas on one side only; place one tortilla, buttered side down, in a 2-qt. round casserole. Spoon about 1/2 cup of meat mixture on the tortilla, then sprinkle with about 1/3 cup cheese. Repeat layers, ending with cheese. Pour water around the sides of casserole (not over the top). Cover and bake at 400° for 20 minutes or until heated through. Let stand 5 minutes before cutting. **Yield:** 4-6 servings.

■ ■ ■

Easy Taco Salad

Faye Shaw, Medicine Hat, Alberta

This salad goes over well at any social function. (Teenagers just love it!) I usually double the recipe because it disappears so fast.

            1 pound ground beef
            1 package (1-1/4 ounces) taco seasoning
            1 medium head lettuce, shredded
            2 medium tomatoes, seeded and chopped
            1 cup bottled Catalina dressing
            4 to 5 cups corn chips, crushed
            2 cups (8 ounces) shredded cheddar cheese

In a skillet, brown ground beef; drain well. Stir in taco seasoning. Combine beef, lettuce, tomatoes, dressing, corn chips and cheese in a large serving bowl; toss well to mix. Serve immediately. **Yield:** 6-8 servings.

> **TEX-MEX MEALS.** Pictured at left from top to bottom: Fiesta Surprise, Mexican Pasta Bake and Layered Tortilla Pie (all recipes on this page).

INDEX

Meatballs in Potato Cups, 46
Meatballs with Rice, 44
Midwest Meatball Casserole, 41
Oven Porcupines, 47
Poached Meatballs in Lemon
    Sauce, 70
Snappy Cocktail Meatballs, 5
Spaghetti Con Carne, 81
Spicy Party Meatballs, 6
Swedish Meatballs, 51
Sweet-and-Sour Meatballs, 7, 69
Unstuffed Cabbage, 77

MEAT LOAVES

Apple-Raisin Meat Loaf, 31
Barbecue Meat Loaf, 30
Busy-Day Meat Loaf, 34
Carrot Meat Loaf, 32
Cheddar Loaf, 31
Classic Meat Loaf, 35
Company Meat Loaf, 27
Country Meat Loaf, 30
Creole Meat Loaf, 30
Crisscross Meat Loaf, 32
Curried Meat Loaf, 29
Deluxe Meat Loaf, 27
Depression Meat Loaf, 34
Favorite Meat Loaf, 28
Frosted Meat Loaf, 28
Golden Secret Meat Loaf, 29
Grandma's Meat Loaf, 28
Juicy Italian Meat Loaf, 29
Marilyn's Meat Loaf, 30
Matchless Meat Loaf, 31
McIntosh Meat Loaf, 29
Meat-and-Potato Patties, 34
Meat Loaf Cordon Bleu, 27
Meat Loaves with Pesto Sauce, 35
Meat Muffins, 28
Mexican Meat Loaf Roll, 32
Mini Meat Loaves, 35
Mozzarella Meat Whirl, 35
Pizza Loaf, 31
Potato Meat Loaf, 27
Pot Roast Meat Loaf, 32
Saucy Meat Loaves, 28
Stuffed Meat Loaf, 34
Tomato-Rice Meatballs, 34
Vegetable Meat Loaf, 31

MEAT PIES
(also see Pizza)

Beef and Cabbage Pie, 63
Beef Biscuits, 62
Beef Crescent Loaf, 55
Beef Pastry Pockets, 67
Bierocks, 60
Burgers for a Bunch, 16
Broccoli Beef Pie, 60
Cheeseburger Quiche, 65
Cornish Pasties, 65

Country Hamburger Pie, 63
French Meat Pie, 67
Italian Vegetable Hot Dish, 63
Layered Tortilla Pie, 95
Mashed Potato Pie, 62
Meat-and-Potato Quiche, 63
Mexican Pie, 93
Priazzo, 59
Spaghetti Pie, 60
Spinach Beef Pie, 60
Sausage Bread, 66
Taco Crescents, 59
Tamale Pie, 83
Topsy-Turvy Pie, 66
Upside-Down Meat Pie, 65
Wagon Wheel Turnovers, 66

MEXICAN DISHES

Acapulco Delight, 84
Beef, Rice and Chili Casserole, 93
Beefy Enchiladas, 84
Cheesy Tortilla Bake, 85
Chilaquilas, 6
Chili 'n' Cheese Enchiladas, 92
Chili con Queso Dip, 6
Chili Relleno Casserole, 93
Cornmeal Empanadas, 84
Easy Taco Salad, 95
Enchilada Casserole, 84
Enchilada Lasagna, 89
Enchilada Torte, 92
Fiesta Appetizers, 7
Fiesta Surprise, 95
Fold-Over Tortilla Bake, 87
Giant Empanadas, 92
Hamburger Chilaquiles, 89
Layered Tortilla Pie, 95
Meatball Chili with Dumplings, 83
Mexican Corn Bread, 88
Mexican Lasagna, 85
Mexican Meat Loaf Roll, 32
Mexican Pasta Bake, 95
Mexican Pie, 93
Navajo Tacos, 92
Pronto Pinwheels, 87
South of the Border Dip, 7
South-of-the-Border Stew, 88
Southwest Skillet Supreme, 89
Sour Cream Chili Bake, 88
Taco Casserole, 85
Taco Crescents, 59
Taco Burgers, 15
Taco Joes, 11
Taco Soup, 9
Taco-Stuffed Potatoes, 70
Taco Tartlets, 7
Tacos Deluxe, 87
Tamale Pie, 83
Terrific Taco Salad, 83
Texas Enchiladas, 88
Texican Rice Salad, 89
Tex-Mex Casserole, 88

PASTA DISHES
(also see Lasagna)

Baked Mostaccioli, 55
Baked Ziti with Fresh Tomatoes, 50
Beef Florentine, 46
Beef Pastitsio, 49
Cannelloni, 38
Cheese 'n' Pasta in a Pot, 39
Chuck Wagon Mac, 47
Crunchy Beef Bake, 46
Curly Noodle Dinner, 71
Italian Stuffed Shells, 54
Macaroni with Beef and Beans, 78
Manicotti, 50
Marzetti, 49
Mexican Pasta Bake, 95

PIZZA

Cheesy Herb Pizza, 62
Crazy Crust Pizza, 67
Different Pizza, 66
Old-World Pizza, 59
Pour Pizza, 62
Stuffed Pizza, 67
Zesty Potato Pizza, 59
Zucchini Pizza, 65

POTATOES

Autumn Soup, 25
Baked Potatoes with Chili, 71
Beef and Bacon Chowder, 17
Beef and Cabbage Pie, 63
Beef and Mashed Potato
    Casserole, 47
Beef and Potato Casserole, 44
Beef Barley Soup, 19
Camper's Special, 75
Cheeseburger Broccoli
    Chowder, 15
Cheesy Beef Dinner, 42
Cornish Pasties, 65
French Meat Pie, 67
Frosted Meat Loaf, 28
German Vegetable Soup, 10
Green Chili, 22
Hamburger Chowder, 16
Hamburger Florentine Soup, 20
Hamburger Stew, 80
Hearty Hamburger Soup, 22

POTATOES *(continued)*

Hobo Knapsacks, 39
Mashed Potato Pie, 62
Meat-and-Potato Casserole, 37
Meat-and-Potato Patties, 34
Meat-and-Potato Quiche, 63
Meat-and-Potato Squares, 51
Meatball Stew, 77
Meatballs in Potato Cups, 46
Pizza Potato Toppers, 78
Poor Man's Dinner, 42
Pot Roast Meat Loaf, 32
Potato Burgers, 24
Potato Lasagna, 55
Potato Meat Loaf, 27
Potato Pizza Hot Dish, 39
Shepherd's Pie, 57
Six-Layer Dinner, 81
16th-Street Stew, 81
Skillet Casserole, 39
Spicy Potato Soup, 19
Taco-Stuffed Potatoes, 70
Tater-Topped Casserole, 42
Zesty Potato Pizza, 59

RICE

Beef and Wild Rice Casserole, 49
Beef Fried Rice, 71
Beef, Rice and Chili Casserole, 93
Cabbage Rolls, 57
Calico Chili, 14
Calico Main Dish Soup, 16
Country Hamburger Pie, 63
Garden Skillet Supper, 78
German Skillet Meal, 78
Jumble Lala, 38
Meatballs with Rice, 44
Mexican Pie, 93
Mock Filet Mignon, 41
Serbian Stuffed Cabbage, 70
Spanish Rice, 74
Stuffed Roast Pepper Soup, 9
Texican Rice Salad, 89
Tomato-Rice Meatballs, 34
Western Hash, 74

SALISBURY STEAK

Salisbury Sauerbraten, 38
Salisbury Steak with Mushroom
   Sauce, 37

SANDWICHES
(also see Hamburgers)

Beef and Cheese Loaf, 24

Beef Stroganoff Sandwich, 19
Curried Beef Pita Pockets, 25
Easy Calzone, 24
"Long Boy" Cheeseburgers, 14
Pizza Buns, 25
Pumpkin Sloppy Joes, 20
Sicilian Burgers, 15
Sloppy Joes, 16
Stromboli, 14
Taco Joes, 11
Tasty Beef Sandwiches, 25

SKILLETS/STIR-FRYS

Black-Eyed Peas Skillet Dinner, 80
Camper's Special, 75
Chop Suey, 71
East-West Stir-Fry, 74
Eggplant Skillet Dinner, 80
Garden Skillet Supper, 78
German Skillet Meal, 78
Hamburger Stroganoff, 69
Haystacks with Cheese Sauce, 80
Six-Layer Dinner, 81
Southwest Zucchini Skillet, 81
Spanish Rice, 74
Western Hash, 74

SOUPS
(also see Chili and Chowder)

Autumn Soup, 25
Beef Barley Soup, 19
Broccoli, Hamburger and Cheese
   Soup, 23
Cabbage Soup, 17
Calico Main Dish Soup, 16
Chicken Escarole Soup with
   Meatballs, 24
German Vegetable Soup, 10
Ham, Beef and Bacon Soup, 23
Hamburger Florentine Soup, 20
Hamburger Vegetable Soup, 14
Hearty Hamburger Soup, 22
Hearty Steak Soup, 17
Meatball Vegetable Soup, 10
Minestrone, 11
Minestrone Mix-Up, 19

Pizza Soup, 20
Prairie Bean Soup, 17
Quick Vegetable Beef Soup, 25
Soup in a Hurry, 11
Spicy Potato Soup, 19
Stuffed Roast Pepper Soup, 9
Taco Soup, 9
Three-Bean Soup, 11

SPAGHETTI SAUCE

Herbed Italian Meat Sauce, 78
Spaghetti Con Carne, 81
Spaghetti Sauce, 75
Spaghetti Squash with Meat
   Sauce, 69

SPINACH

Beef Florentine, 46
Cannelloni, 38
East-West Stir-Fry, 74
Fiesta Surprise, 95
Hamburger Florentine Soup, 20
Meat Loaves with Pesto Sauce, 35
Minestrone Mix-Up, 19
Spinach Beef Pie, 60
Stuffed Pizza, 67

SQUASH

Baked Potatoes with Chili, 71
Beef-Stuffed Acorn Squash, 41
Curried Beef Pita Pockets, 25
Southwest Zucchini Skillet, 81
Spaghetti Squash with Meat
   Sauce, 69
Stuffed Zucchini, 55
Zucchini Garden Casserole, 41
Zucchini Italiano, 49
Zucchini Pizza, 65
Zucchini Pizza Casserole, 51

STEWS

Aunt Fran's Goulash, 75
Beef and Barley Mulligan, 77
Hamburger Stew, 80
Lentil Stew, 74
Meatball Stew, 77
16th-Street Stew, 81
South-of-the-Border Stew, 88